"Inspiring and comprehensive real-life examples make this book an excellent and valuable 'how-to' guide for applying this evidence-based practice in the education of preschool-aged children with autism. This should be highly recommended reading for parents, teachers, and all healthcare professionals dedicated to improving the quality of life of these children."

—*Dr Christos Nikopoulos, BCBA-D, Lecturer, School of Health Sciences and Social Care, Brunel University, UK, and co-author of* Video Modelling and Behaviour Analysis: A Guide for Teaching Social Skills to Children with Autism

"The methods described in this book have been life changing for my three-year-old son and our family. We started with appropriate play videos, moved to self-care routines (getting dressed, brushing teeth, haircuts), focused sharply on safety videos (holding hands, staying with a parent), and are now using video modeling to help with his transition to pre-school. The videos have provided our son with the visual and audio aids that he needs and craves in order to be successful. The changes in his behavior have been nothing short of amazing."

—*Wendy Gilbertson, parent of a child with autism, Minnesota*

"Sarah Murray and Brenna Noland's book is timely as the use of technology to support the learning of individuals with autism spectrum disorders has rapidly grown due to the increased availability and decreased cost of technological equipment. This book, written by practitioners in the field, provides actual case studies that demonstrate how to realistically use video modeling. The case studies include a variety of skills and routines across multiple settings including home, community, and school. If you are thinking about implementing video modeling in your practice with young children, this book is a valuable tool."

—*L. Lynn Stansberry Brusnahan, PhD, Associate Professor, School of Education, University of St. Thomas, Minnesota, and 2012 recipient of the Dr. Cathy Pratt Autism Professional of the Year Award from the Autism Society of America*

"One of the most challenging aspects of parenting two children with (very different) autism spectrum disorders is the variety of opinions on methods of treatment; from ABA to DIR/Floortime to RDI, as parents we seek to try anything that might help us navigate this uncharted territory. The beauty of video modeling is that it works across the spectrum in teaching our children appropriate behaviors in a way that makes sense and brings results. Over the course of the last six years our family has been blessed to work with both Brenna Noland and Sarah Murray, and their wonderful book is a clear 'how-to' manual for addressing challenging behaviors and helping our children. So straightforward and helpful, this book will be my first gift to parents of newly-diagnosed children with ASD."

—*Christina Kellaway-Loescher, mother to Shay (8, autism) and Kitty (10, Asperger syndrome), Minnesota*

"As a special education teacher and autism specialist, I find this book to be an invaluable resource. The user-friendly format is an easy read, and it is full of practical strategies that can be used immediately, without a lot of preparation. I have utilized video modeling for individual skills as well as group routines, and the results are impressive."

—*Christina Reynolds, autism specialist, Prior Lake-Savage Area Schools, Minnesota*

# VIDEO MODELING
# FOR YOUNG CHILDREN
# WITH AUTISM SPECTRUM DISORDERS

# VIDEO MODELING FOR YOUNG CHILDREN WITH AUTISM SPECTRUM DISORDERS

## A Practical Guide for Parents and Professionals

*Sarah Murray and Brenna Noland*

Jessica Kingsley *Publishers*
London and Philadelphia

Permission for the photographs were kindly granted
by the families of the children featured.

First published in 2013
by Jessica Kingsley Publishers
116 Pentonville Road
London N1 9JB, UK
and
400 Market Street, Suite 400
Philadelphia, PA 19106, USA

*www.jkp.com*

**Library of Congress Cataloging in Publication Data**
Video modeling for young children with autism spectrum disorders : a practical guide
for parents and
professionals
     p. cm.
Includes bibliographical references and index.
ISBN 978-1-84905-900-8 (alk. paper)
1. Autistic children--Education--Audio-visual aids.
LC4717.V54 2013
371.94--dc23
                    2012013509

**British Library Cataloguing in Publication Data**
A CIP catalogue record for this book is available from the British Library

ISBN 978 1 84905 900 8
eISBN 978 0 85700 638 7

Printed and bound in Great Britain

*In memory of Bill and Artis Stensrud,*
*who gave me the gift of an adventurous childhood.*
*To Grace and Evie,*
*who give me so much joy. I love you!*

Sarah


*To my parents, Dave and Renée Noland,*
*and to my grandparents, Jack and Rita Lamoureux,*
*thank you for your continued love, encouragement, and support.*
*I couldn't have done it without you guys.*
*I love you all SO much.*

Brenna

# CONTENTS

# ACKNOWLEDGMENTS

We would like to acknowledge the Minnetonka Public School District for initiating our journey into the world of video modeling. It was this district's Early Childhood Special Education (ECSE) program that sent us to our first training on video modeling and shared in our excitement regarding the endless possibilities that video modeling could afford. We would like to thank the coordinator of ECSE services in Minnetonka for supporting our use of video modeling with young children with autism spectrum disorders (ASD) by providing us with all of the necessary materials including everything from the cameras we use to record the raw footage to the iPads we use to play the finished videos back to our students. We would like to thank the technology services in Minnetonka for providing us with training on how to use various editing software, teaching us all about file conversion software and constantly loading our iPads with our newest videos. We would like to thank the staff development department in Minnetonka for sending us to Florida in June 2011 so we could present at a national conference on *Using Technology to Address the Core Deficits in Young Children with ASD*. It was at this conference that we were approached about the possibility of writing our first book. We would like to thank our colleagues within Minnetonka's ECSE program for understanding and supporting our eagerness to teach anything and everything we could think of through video modeling! We truly believe that we wouldn't be here today without all of the support we have received through the Minnetonka Public School District. We are proud to work within such an amazing district. Last, but certainly not least, we would like to thank the families we've worked with over the years for having faith in us as teachers and for being open to trying new things. Thank you!

# INTRODUCTION

The use of visuals with young children with autism spectrum disorders (ASD) is a well-established and commonly used strategy with families and professionals today. The use of technology to support the learning of this population is rapidly growing due to the increased availability and decreased cost of technological equipment. Video modeling takes the use of visuals to the next level by combining a conventional strategy with new technologies to create an even more effective teaching tool. Video modeling allows children to learn new skills by doing something they love... watching movies! These personalized videos highlight specific behaviors that you want the child (i.e., your student, client, or child) to exhibit while demonstrating a specific skill or completing a specific routine. Video modeling allows the child to learn expected behaviors quickly, which allows him to demonstrate skills and complete routines with less hands-on adult support.

Video modeling is not a new teaching strategy. In fact, the use of video modeling to increase the skills of individuals with special needs is supported by a considerable amount of research that has been completed over the past 30 years. Although the efficacy of video modeling with preschool-aged children is reinforced by a growing amount of research, there is a severe lack of research supporting this intervention for use with children under the age of three. One major reason for the lack of research may be due to the average age in which a child is diagnosed with an ASD.

A recent study determined that in the United States the average age of diagnosis was 5.7 years old (Shattuck *et al.* 2009). Another contributing factor to the sparse research including this population could be due to the setting in which their services are primarily provided. Researchers have more control over the environment and can observe and document behaviors more readily within a small therapy room; however, most children under the age of three receive the majority of their services within the home setting.

While the current research may not confirm this, we have found video modeling to be an effective strategy for many young children with ASD under the age of three. We have even found this to be an effective strategy for some children prior to their second birthdays. We have been using various types of video modeling to support the development of young children with ASD over the past few years and have observed incredible success with children between the ages of 22 months and 7 years. One of the greatest benefits of video modeling that we have observed is the speed in which the children are able to acquire new skills. We have seen children master skills in a matter of weeks that used to take children of similar ability levels up to a few months to learn. Our major successes include the following:

- Increased attention toward an activity.

- Increased social interaction skills (e.g., responding to name, greetings, turn-taking).

- Increased basic functional play skills.

- Increased creative play skills.

- Increased immediate imitation of simple actions with objects.

- Increased independence within a variety of daily routines (e.g., toileting, dressing).

- Increased ease of transitions between activities.

- Increased amount of functional language used during daily routines.

- Increased independent initiation of activities.

- Increased positive affect during a specific activity.

- Increased appropriate tool use (e.g., spoon, pencil, scissors).

- Increased ability to remain safe (e.g., responding to safety directions, holding hands).

- Decreased anxiety surrounding activities (e.g., riding a bike, going to the dentist).

- Decreased inappropriate behaviors during daily routines.

This book will provide you with an in-depth description of three different types of video modeling including Basic Video Modeling (BVM), Video Self-Modeling (VSM), and Point-of-view Video Modeling (PVM). Each type of video modeling differs slightly based on its specific advantages as well as the way in which each type of video is created. Each type is similar in that it allows the child to learn in a motivating and visual manner, which is imperative when working with children with ASD. Following the description of each strategy, you will be provided with step-by-step instructions describing how to create a video to target a change in a child's behavior, which will increase his ability to demonstrate a skill or complete a routine. The instructions include everything from choosing a skill or routine to target and the equipment needed, to recording, editing, and showing the video.

If you are craving more details after reading through the descriptions and steps, you are in luck! Following the step-by-step instructions you will find comprehensive case studies that will build upon what you have already learned and will provide you with all the information you need to hit the ground running. (Yes... you will be creating videos and successfully increasing children's skills in no time!) Each case study is a true story derived from our experience with using BVM, VSM, and PVM with young children with ASD. Each of the studies will provide you with the following information: (1) a thorough description of a child with ASD; (2) a summary of the video used with that child including what skill it targeted and how it was made; (3) a description of what was done once the video was completed including how the video was shown to the child and what we did following the child's viewing; (4) the child's outcomes in regards to the skill being targeted; and (5) information pertaining to how we faded the use of the video and if the child was able to generalize his learned behaviors.

We wrote this book while keeping the following target audience in mind: anyone who interacts with a young child with ASD on a regular basis. The information in this book will be extremely useful to the following individuals:

- Parents

- Other caregivers including extended family members, nannies, daycare providers, etc.

- Preschool teachers

- Early intervention teachers (those who serve infants and toddlers with special needs from birth through two years of age and their families)

- Special education teachers (those who serve children with special needs ages three and older)

- Specialized therapists including speech and language pathologists, occupational therapists, physical therapists, autism specialists, etc.

- Mental health practitioners

As a parent (or other primary caregiver), you will learn how easy it is to turn those dreaded daily routines (e.g., dressing, meals, bath time) into enjoyable activities for the entire family just by increasing one or more of your child's skills through video modeling. You will learn how to increase your child's ability to participate in activities in the community such as playing at the park, visiting the doctor, or getting a haircut. You will also learn more about effective ways to target your child's skills at school. Although you are not the one providing your child's services within his classroom, you are viewed as an important part of your child's educational team and your input is invaluable. After reading this book, you will be better able to help your child's team problem solve tricky behaviors or figure out how to address a lack of progress in one certain area within the classroom setting.

We understand that as a daycare provider or preschool teacher it is not your job to provide therapy to young children with ASD. We also understand that you are often in charge of a large number of children and are provided with minimal support. Although you may not use these strategies to target the growth of a specific skill (e.g., appropriate grip on a pencil), you may find it helpful to use these strategies to increase a child's independence within daily routines. As the child with ASD improves in his ability to put on outdoor clothes (e.g., coat, hat, mittens) or to remain engaged in quiet play during rest time with less adult support, you will be more able to spread your attention and support across all of the children you care for. In fact, you will probably find that *all* children who are receiving your care (with or without special needs) will benefit from video modeling.

As early intervention teachers, special education teachers, specialized therapists, and/or mental health practitioners, you will learn how to use video modeling in order to increase children's abilities across all areas of development. You will learn how easy it is to use video modeling in any setting in which you serve young children with ASD (e.g., home, community classroom designed for children without special needs, special education classrooms, private therapy centers) and how to make successful videos for children of varying abilities. You will be pleased to find just how well video modeling can support and even enhance your current teaching strategies. You will also learn about the research that has been conducted that proves that video modeling is an evidence-based practice.

Following the chapters on video modeling, you will find an additional chapter describing other ways that video-recording devices can be used to support the development of young children with ASD. One of the strategies that will be discussed includes the use of reflective practices to target an increase in self-awareness, both in children with ASD as well as those who interact with them. Children with ASD are often not aware of their own behaviors and how their behaviors may be affecting those around them such as their caregivers, siblings, peers, etc. This lack of awareness is also true when it comes to those working with young children with ASD. When an adult is busy supporting a child during any given activity or routine, it is difficult for the adult to see how their actions (e.g., voice volume, reactions to behaviors, speed, level of support) are affecting the child. Children with ASD as well as the adults who support them can benefit greatly from watching video footage of themselves in action. Other uses of video-recording devices that will be discussed include targeting an increase in self-monitoring skills, adult training, progress monitoring, and lesson extension activities.

**Note to the reader:** While we are aware that ASD does not discriminate between genders (although males are affected more than females), we have chosen to use *he* rather than *he or she* throughout each chapter in order to add to your ease of reading. We thank you for your understanding and we hope you enjoy the book!

CHAPTER

# 1

# BASIC VIDEO MODELING (BVM)

Basic Video Modeling (BVM) is a teaching strategy in which the learner watches a video of an actor other than himself appropriately demonstrating a specific skill or routine. The goal is to target a change in a learner's behavior, which will increase his ability to successfully demonstrate a skill or routine. Behavior refers to "any change in an entity with respect to its surroundings" (Bigelow, Roenblueth, and Wiener 1943, p.18). This means that behavior is *everything* a child does in response to his environment (the physical environment as well as other people), not just the naughty stuff. In order to best distinguish between good and bad behaviors throughout this book, we use terminology derived from Michelle Garcia Winner's Social Thinking curriculum. According to Winner, "expected behaviors" refer to any behavior that is "socially appropriate," while "unexpected behaviors" refer to any behavior that is "socially inappropriate" (Winner 2007, p.160). Unexpected behaviors will typically make a child stand out in an unusual way. The behavior of *remaining seated* could be an expected or unexpected behavior depending upon the context in which it is observed. Remaining seated in a chair while completing an art project would be considered an expected behavior, whereas remaining seated on the floor during gym time would be an unexpected behavior.

Examples of expected behaviors that you could target using BVM may include approaching a teacher using walking feet (as opposed to running), calling the teacher's name using an appropriate voice volume, and calmly waiting for the teacher's response. Targeting an increase in these expected behaviors will have a positive impact on the child's ability to demonstrate the skill of gaining his teacher's attention. A BVM video highlighting the previous expected behaviors will also work toward decreasing many unexpected behaviors including yelling the teacher's name from across the room or running toward the teacher and pulling on the teacher's arm when the child needs something.

BVM is an evidence-based practice that has been proven to be an effective strategy in teaching and shaping skills and behaviors in children with autism spectrum disorders (ASD). In a study completed by Charlop-Christy, Le, and Freeman (2000), the effectiveness of using BVM to teach developmental skills to young children with ASD was compared to the effectiveness of using In Vivo modeling to teach these same skills. In Vivo modeling is defined as the learner observing a live model performing the target behavior. The results suggest that BVM leads to faster acquisition of skills than In Vivo modeling and effectively promotes generalization (i.e., the demonstration of the targeted skill in different settings or with different materials). The researchers suggest that the results may be due to video modeling's motivating and attention maintaining qualities. Corbett and Abdullah (2005) define characteristics of learners with ASD that help to explain why video modeling is particularly effective with this group of learners in their study entitled "Video Modeling: Why Does It Work for Children with Autism?" The specific characteristics include: (1) a preference for visual stimuli and visual instruction; (2) an avoidance of face-to-face interactions; and (3) an ability to process visual information more readily than verbal information.

In our BVM videos, we typically use the learner's parents, siblings, peers, or teachers as the actors; there are many possible choices, however. The actor could be a person who is already able to demonstrate the skill independently, a person who can demonstrate the skill with some adult support, or a person who needs training in order to demonstrate the skill. If, prior to filming, the actor is provided with training regarding what to do and say during the recording process, there may be no need for editing of the raw footage. This inherently makes BVM videos easy to create because it decreases the amount of editing that is required. Another benefit of BVM is that the videos can typically be used with multiple learners who are working on the same, targeted skill. For example, a video created of a boy washing his hands can be used with any child who is learning to complete the same hand washing routine.

BVM can be used to teach a wide variety of skills across all developmental domains including communication, cognition, motor, social-emotional, and adaptive. We have found BVM to be extremely effective at targeting independence within daily routines such as washing hands, dressing, and tidying away toys. We have also found that BVM is particularly effective at increasing a learner's ability to remain calm during transitions. Watching a video of another person's successful transition, such as finishing dinner and then going up to take a bath, allows the learner to know what the conclusion of the current activity looks like and what to expect next, thus increasing his knowledge of the transition and increasing his self-confidence in his ability to complete the routine. BVM is also helpful in increasing successful participation in and decreasing anxiety associated with unfamiliar activities such as dental exams, haircuts, and doctor visits. Watching a video of an unfamiliar event inevitably makes the event more familiar, less scary, and less stressful. We have also used BVM to teach various social and communication skills from simple skills such as asking a peer for a turn during play and using a person's name to get her attention, to more complicated skills such as playing a board game with a peer.

## STEPS TO BASIC VIDEO MODELING

We have identified ten steps that are important to follow when using BVM with young children with ASD. These steps are described in detail below. While the process may seem overwhelming at first, you will find that your ability to move through the steps quickly increases with each video you create.

## Step One: Identify a skill or routine that you would like to target

In identifying a skill or routine that you would like to target, it is important to keep in mind general child development as well as the level at which the child is currently functioning. The targeted skill or routine must only include behaviors that can be expected of a similarly aged child and must be within the child's reach. For example, it may be appropriate to teach a four-year-old child to wash his hands independently but it would not be appropriate to expect him to sit and attend to a 45-minute lesson.

## Step Two: Identify and assemble the equipment needed

Before beginning to make your BVM video, you should identify and gather all the equipment you need. In order to create a BVM video, you will need a video-recording device and a way to play the video back to the child. You may also need editing software. Many video-recording devices come with built-in editing software. Most computer software bundles come with video-editing software such as Windows Movie Maker (PC) or iMovie (Mac). While most BVM videos do not require editing to depict a positive example of the targeted skill or routine, many parents and educators choose to edit out background noise or add background music. If you are the actor in the video, you will also need a tripod or another person to operate the camera. You will also need to think about how you will show the video to the child. The current options for playing back a video include a television, computer, portable DVD player, interactive whiteboard, electronic tablet, smartphone, or the actual video-recording device. These options are changing quickly as technology advances! The way you choose to show it to the child will often depend on where you show the video. For example, you may want to have the child watch the video in his home and also in his classroom at school. How you choose to have your child watch the video will determine what equipment you will need for saving the video such as a DVD or USB flash drive.

## Step Three: Complete a task analysis of the skill or routine and collect baseline data

When planning to create a BVM video, it is important to complete a task analysis of the skill or routine as well as to collect baseline data. Task analysis sounds daunting but it actually just involves deconstructing the skill or routine to identify its smallest elements (each expected behavior). For example, a child's school arrival routine may involve eight separate steps, including: entering the classroom, walking to the cubby area, locating his cubby by his printed name, taking off his backpack, hanging his backpack in the correct cubby, unzipping his jacket, taking off his jacket, and hanging the jacket in the correct cubby. Before you create the video or begin trying to make changes to the child's behavior or ability to demonstrate the skill, it is a good idea to collect baseline data. This simply means observing the child to see what he is currently able to do. It is important to determine if there are any elements of the target skill or routine that the child can already demonstrate independently. If you find that the child can complete any steps of the skill without adult support that come at the beginning or at the end of the routine, it may not be necessary to include these steps in the video.

## Step Four: Make a plan for the filming of the video

Before filming, we suggest making a plan for filming the video. You will first need to decide which type of video modeling video you will create. See Appendix A for more information on how to choose the type of video modeling that best matches the child and the target skill or routine. Once you have determined the type of video you will create, we suggest you write an outline and a script that includes everything the actor will do and say in the video from start to finish. See Appendix B for sample outlines for common skills and routines.

## Step Five: Record the video

This is the fun step...recording the video! How you proceed with recording a BVM video will depend, to some extent, on the age and ability level of the actor. If the actor is an adult, you should be able to record the entire video in one continuous and errorless take that will, in turn, require little or no editing. When using a child or children as actor(s), this is not always the case. When working with children, it is often helpful to role-play and complete a few practice runs before filming. It is important to remember that a child actor does not necessarily need to be able to independently complete the entire skill or routine prior to filming. You can always record the child actor performing the skill in smaller increments. This would allow you to provide additional training and support to the child actor in between each take; however, it will also require you to complete additional editing.

We have found that some learners respond better to certain actors. The research on model preference and effectiveness is inconclusive. Bandura (1977) found that a child is more motivated to attend to a model that is similar to the child in physical characteristics, gender, and age. However, in a study by Mechling and Moser (2010) that examined model preferences in middle school students with ASD, the results were less conclusive. These two researchers found that *collectively* there was minimal difference between the three model choices (videos of themselves, a peer, or a familiar adult performing a skill). However, they did find that there were *individual* preferences for models that were not necessarily consistent with the models the others preferred. With these results in mind, it may require a bit of trial and error to determine what type of actor the child responds to best. The child may respond best to a same-aged child actor of the same gender, to a same-aged child actor of a different gender, or to an adult actor. You may also need to determine if the child responds better to a familiar or unfamiliar actor.

In the next step, you will learn how to edit your raw footage in order to create a BVM video; one of the advantages of BVM, however, is that editing is not always needed. Having said that, coming up with raw footage that does not require editing takes a bit of planning. For example, a BVM video to teach the child to imitate an adult's simple motor action of clapping hands could be created in a few different ways, each requiring different amounts of editing. In one method, you could record clips of the adult actor clapping his own hands and then film separate clips of the child actor clapping hands. These clips would then need to be spliced together during editing. In a different method, however, this video could be created in one shot that requires no editing. This would be accomplished by making sure that both the adult actor and the child actor were within the camera's frame while filming the clapping or by first recording the adult actor clapping his hands and then panning the camera to the child actor who would then clap his hands.

## Step Six: Edit the video footage

As noted in Step Two, before beginning the filming process you need to identify how you will edit your raw footage. If you are using the built-in editing software on your video-recording device, you will be given the option to download this software onto your computer when you plug the camera into the computer. Some cameras allow the user to edit footage directly on the camera itself. Other editing options include using computer software such as Windows Movie Maker (PC) or iMovie (Mac), which are sold separately and are not associated with any specific camera.

Depending on your familiarity with the software and with technology in general, the first video you create may take a long time to edit. Do not get discouraged. Given time and familiarity with your software and with the editing process, you will get much faster at creating impressive videos! The pitfall in which many parents and educators find themselves is trying to make their videos too professional looking. We have found that children do not notice most of the bells and whistles of "fancy" videos, including impressive fading between shots and perfect transitions. More importantly, professional-looking BVM videos that take a lot of time to create are not necessarily any more effective than less sophisticated BVM videos. Have fun and remember that you can always tweak the video if your first try is not as effective as you had hoped. The length of the completed video will depend upon the child's attention span, although we recommend that videos are no longer than three minutes, as a good rule of thumb.

No matter what software you choose to use, the editing process is similar. Listed below are the seven steps for editing BVM videos. They do not necessarily need to be completed in this order. Additionally, not all seven steps will be needed in editing every BVM video.

1. Import the raw footage into the editing software. There are several ways to accomplish this and it will vary depending on your software.

2. Splice the raw footage to include only the parts that you want in the final video. Remember, you can mute any unwanted sounds such as off-screen directions to the actors and distracting background noises, so you do not necessarily need to discard these parts.

3. You will need to decide if you want to use any still shots within the video. Still shots are a powerful tool frequently used to highlight a skill. For example, in a BVM video that teaches a child to clean up after snack time, a still shot could be used to highlight putting a napkin in the garbage. To add a still shot you can either use a photo taken with a camera or use a single frame from your raw footage.

4. Mute any unwanted sounds. Undesirable sounds may include distracting background noises and off-screen directions to the actors.

5. Add voice-over narration. Narration is useful in highlighting specific steps, rules, or expectations. It is often helpful to add narration to describe what an onscreen actor has said as well as to highlight the salient feature of a statement or action. Many children with ASD have difficulty discerning the relevant information in an interaction or behavior. Narration can take out the guesswork. For example, in a

video created to teach cleaning up after a snack, the narrator could say, "Look! Johnny put his napkin in the garbage." Even though the video showed Johnny putting the napkin in the garbage, the narration highlights this action to make sure the learner does not miss it.

6. Add background music. Music is another powerful element in a BVM video. It can be used to demonstrate that the targeted skill or routine is an enjoyable activity. Music can also increase the viewer's enjoyment while watching the video, therefore increasing the likelihood that he will attend to the entire video. We have found it important to match the tone and pace of the music to the activity in the video. For example, in a video created to teach a bedtime routine, a slow-paced song would be appropriate. In a video created to decrease the anxiety associated with getting a haircut, a calm song would be best. We suggest instrumental music for most videos so the words of the song do not interfere with the message of the video. An exception would be if the words of the music added to the message of the video (e.g., a "haircuts are fun" song in the previously mentioned video). There are many websites that offer free music and sounds that can be downloaded for use in videos (e.g., Freeplaymusic.com and Beemp3.com).

7. Save the video for playback. As mentioned earlier, how you save your finished video will depend on how you plan to show it to the child. Some options include saving it to a USB flash drive, directly onto a computer or tablet, or onto a DVD.

## Step Seven: Show the video to the child

After you have created the video and saved it for playback, you can show it to the child. Whether you are showing the video in the child's home, out in the community, or in a classroom, there are many options for video playback. These options include a television, computer, portable DVD player, interactive whiteboard, electronic tablet, smartphone, etc. To increase the effectiveness of the video, it is important to give the child the opportunity to watch the video in its entirety without interruption. Making comments to the child (or any other attempts at social engagement) during viewing will most likely distract the child and have a negative impact on his learning at this time. While it may be easy to control your behavior during the viewing, it may not be as easy to control the environment in which the viewing is occurring. Distraction-free viewing opportunities might be easier to accomplish in the child's home. If the child is watching the video at school, it might be best to play it on a portable device in a quiet area of the classroom or in the hall. An option for watching the video in a noisy classroom is to have the child wear headphones.

Every child is different and may benefit from different frequencies of viewing. Some may need to watch the video every day, while others may demonstrate progress when only given a few opportunities to watch the video each week. If possible, allow the child to watch the video immediately prior to practicing the skill. If this adds one extra transition that is difficult for the child or is not possible, the video can be shown at a different time. You may find that some children benefit from practicing the skill immediately following the viewing, while other children's performances are not affected by a significant amount of time passing between the viewing and the practice.

## Step Eight: Facilitate skill development following the viewing of the video

It is extremely important to recognize that you will still need to facilitate the child's skills even when using BVM videos. BVM is not necessarily a quick fix and will not always immediately increase the child's ability to perform a certain skill or routine. No matter what kind of progress the child makes, it is important to continue to support his development of new skills using other effective strategies as well. No matter how incredibly effective BVM can be, we do not recommend using it as a stand-alone intervention.

## Step Nine: Monitor progress to determine if changes need to be made

As the child continues to watch his BVM video, we highly recommend that you monitor his progress to determine if you need to make any changes. Record data on the child's ability to demonstrate all expected behaviors while demonstrating the skill or routine that you are targeting. This will provide you with concrete evidence to look back upon when determining whether or not sufficient progress has been made. Again, we know this may sound daunting. Like taking baseline data, it merely means watching the child and jotting down notes of what he is able to do. See Appendix C for sample data sheets that may be useful to you during this step.

## Step Ten: Problem solve if progress is slow

If you find that the child's progress is slower than you expected, you should look for all possible reasons for this. There are many things to consider if the child is not progressing as you would have hoped. Here are several questions you should ask yourself when trying to identify a reason for slow progress.

- Are you showing the video often enough?

- Is there a better time within the child's day that the video could be shown?

- Is the environment in which the child is watching the video too distracting?

- Is the video too long?

- Does the skill or routine that you are targeting include too many steps or are the expected behaviors too far out of the child's reach?

- Would the child benefit more from watching a video that includes an actor of a different gender, age, or relationship to him?

Begin making changes by adjusting only one variable, such as the frequency in which the video is shown, and then continue to monitor the child's progress. If you make too many changes at once it will be difficult to determine what variable made the biggest impact. The knowledge you gain in problem solving why a BVM video was not as effective as you had hoped will be useful information when creating subsequent videos.

## BASIC VIDEO MODELING CASE STUDIES

The following five case studies are actual examples that demonstrate how we have used BVM with children and families whom we have worked with. The case studies are arranged in ascending order by the age of the child, from two up to five years. They address a variety of skills and routines across multiple settings including home, community, and school.

## DAVID (TWO YEARS OLD):
## HOLDING HANDS WHILE WALKING
### Child background

At 22 months of age, David was evaluated through his local school district. He qualified for early intervention services under the educational category of ASD. His parents reported that their two biggest concerns were his language development and frequent tantrums. David's evaluation team determined that his expressive language skills were at the low end of average when compared to other children his same age. At that time, he had 18 words that he used consistently throughout his day. David's understanding of language was significantly below average. He was not yet following basic directions that were given multiple times each day including, "Time to eat," and "Time to change diaper." He loved to look at books, but was not yet able to point to familiar pictures when named. David's parents reported that he engaged in up to 30 tantrums each day, each lasting anywhere from a few seconds to ten minutes. His tantrums typically occurred when he was told, "No," or during transitions between activities. All transitions were difficult for David no matter how minor they seemed (e.g., cleaning up the blocks and moving onto playing with cars, playing upstairs with a toy and moving downstairs to play with that same toy, stopping an activity to get his diaper changed). The behaviors observed during his tantrums included dropping to the floor, screaming, crying, throwing, and running away. These behaviors made it impossible for him to participate in any activities outside of his home including playing at the park and grocery shopping. His behaviors even caused his parents to be very apprehensive about carrying out basic daily routines within their home including meals, diaper changes, and baths. David was not yet following basic safety directions and was not successful playing in any unfenced outdoor area without adult support.

Once an effective calm-down routine was established and after transitions within their home were addressed (four months into services), David's parents wanted to work on walking while holding hands. This was a skill that was necessary in order for David to safely participate in a variety of community activities. At just over two years of age, David was not yet demonstrating any foundational skills to walking while holding an adult's hand such as understanding common dangers, following simple directions, and remaining calm during transitions. Prior to video modeling, David was only able to take one or two steps at a time while holding an adult's hand without collapsing to the ground, protesting, and crying.

### Description of the video

A BVM video was created to teach David how to walk near his father while holding onto a walking rope and remaining calm. A walking rope is a short rope with small rings every 10 to 12 inches for children to hold onto. The video was recorded in an empty school hallway and the actors were five female teachers. The video was less than one minute in length and consisted of the actors holding onto the rings and walking down the hall while remaining in single file. During the video, the person filming said, "Walk,

walk, walk," and "Nice walking." No editing was needed for this video to be effective.

## Viewing the video

Because no editing was needed, the video was saved onto the family computer during one of their weekly home visits, just minutes after it was recorded. David watched it for the first time during this visit. It was important for David to watch the video from start to finish without interruption (e.g., no television on in the background, no commenting by an adult). In order to make this happen, David was held in his father's arms while the video played on a laptop situated on the kitchen counter-top. He was held more than a foot away from the counter-top so that he could not reach the computer with his hands or feet. David was very interested in the video and kept his eyes on the screen until the video ended. In order to achieve the most success, David's father and teacher decided that David should watch the video every day, followed by an opportunity to practice the skill. Since David had a difficult time with transitions, it was recommended that the video be viewed in conjunction with the same activities each day (immediately following his breakfast and before playing with toys or after his brother got home from school and before his afternoon snack) so he would start to anticipate what was coming next.

## Facilitating skill development following the video

Following the first viewing, David was prompted to hold onto a ring along with his father and teacher (his father was in front of him and his teacher was behind him). Walking while holding onto the walking rope was first practiced around the kitchen island. His father and teacher modeled the words and phrases heard in the video. When David let go of the rope, an adult led him back to the ring and provided him with physical assistance while saying, "Hold circle." In order to keep him engaged in the activity, the adults sang the ABC's and stomped their feet. At the end of the song, the adults cheered before starting the song again. David's ability to maintain a grasp on the ring was best when paired with singing and stomping. David and his father continued to practice this skill each day after they watched the video. David's older brother often joined in, which turned this activity into an exciting game for David. During his next home visit (seven days later), this skill was practiced outside on the sidewalk following the viewing of the video. Again, his father held onto the ring in front and his teacher held the ring behind him. His ability to hold onto the ring while walking near his father had improved; however, there were many exciting things for him to touch outside (e.g., rocks, leaves, grass, bugs), which made it difficult for him to control his impulses. This skill was practiced a second time after he was given a bucket of rocks to hold onto with his free hand. Holding onto the bucket gave him something to do with his other hand so that both hands had a specific job. His early intervention teacher hoped that this would help him to remain engaged in the activity and decrease his impulsivity.

*Figure 1.1. The walking rope*

## Child outcomes

Within two full weeks of viewing the video and practicing the skill, David was successfully walking more than three blocks at a time while holding onto the walking rope. His father no longer had to sing or stomp in order to keep him engaged and instead could talk about the things they saw outside such as the cars, trees, and birds. If David accidentally dropped the ring, he consistently came back to the rope and grabbed onto the ring without any adult support. He no longer needed to hold onto the bucket. David's father was absolutely thrilled with David's new skill and was excited to practice it in new environments.

## Fading and generalization

After three weeks of watching the video and practicing the skill every day, David was able to walk with an adult while holding hands. His father discovered this after finding himself in a situation in which David needed to hold his hand when the rope was not around. David held his father's hand in a variety of environments including David's school, the grocery store, and on the sidewalk outside their house. David's father reported that David no longer needed to watch the video in order to demonstrate this skill. In his father's eyes, David had passed the ultimate test when he was able to join the family in walking down to the neighborhood playground! His parents were no longer afraid of taking him out in the community, which had a positive effect on the entire family.

# BRYCE (TWO-AND-A-HALF YEARS OLD): RESPONDING TO SAFETY DIRECTIONS
## Child background

Bryce received a medical diagnosis of ASD one month following his second birthday. He had been receiving services through a private clinic and through his local school district since that time. At the age of two-and-a-half, Bryce knew approximately 40 words and spoke primarily in one-word phrases. His ability to follow through with basic one-step directions such as, "Get the book," or "Sit in chair," was inconsistent. Bryce was a very busy boy and required a substantial amount of adult support in order to keep his body safe. He was very impulsive and distractible, which had an impact on his ability to remain engaged in daily routines without a great deal of adult support. His home was cleared of all decorations that he could possibly reach (e.g., vases on shelves, picture frames on tables, clocks) as well as some functional pieces of furniture including kitchen chairs. Bryce craved physical activities such as spinning, jumping, and crashing into soft surfaces; he seemed to benefit from the added sensory input that these actions provided him. His backyard was not conducive to outdoor play because there were too many trees. His front yard had a spacious grassy area and a large driveway, which created a nice outdoor play space. Bryce's mother was not comfortable playing with him in the front yard without extra adult support, however, because of his constant desire to run into the street. Because he was not yet responding to, "Stop!" she needed to be within arm's reach of him at all times. It was impossible for her to accomplish this while also caring for his 14-month-old younger brother. Bryce's mother felt strongly about working on his ability to remain safe while playing in the front yard with less adult support.

## Description of the video

A BVM video was created to increase Bryce's ability to appropriately respond to, "Stop!" when he reached the end of his driveway. The actors in the video were a two-and-a-half-year-old boy and a four-year-old girl. These children were chosen because they were already able to demonstrate this skill without adult support. They were also family members of the person filming, which made scheduling the filming much easier! The video was filmed on the actors' driveway. Prior to filming, a visual stopping point (a long line of square foam mats that connect together like a puzzle) was placed at the end of the driveway. Since Bryce would be less likely to run into the street if engaged in play, some exciting outdoor play items were gathered including bubbles in a spill-proof bottle, chalk, and materials for a car wash (i.e., spray bottle, sponge, bucket, and towel). The chalk was introduced to the actors first and the recording began as they started to play. The person filming was able to verbally direct the actors' actions during play because all of the sound from the raw footage was going to be covered up by music and voice-overs. Every 15 to 30 seconds, one actor was directed to walk down to the end of the driveway and stop when he reached the foam mats. That actor was then directed to come back to the materials and continue playing. This was repeated with each set of materials. A total of approximately ten minutes of video was recorded; however, this footage was edited into a video of just over two minutes. During the editing process, a quiet instrumental song was added into the background. Voice-overs were added so that there was simple narration regarding what the kids were doing (e.g., "Wash car." "Sponge in bucket." "Bubbles go up!" "Draw circle"). As the video showed one of the actors approaching the end of the driveway, the editor recorded her own voice as she said, "Stop!" A still frame of the video was created showing the actor stopped in front of the foam mats in order to emphasize the stopping. The video then continued to show the actor returning to play as the editor added the phrase, "Good stopping!" The finished video showed the following sequence eight times: (1) the actors playing; (2) one actor walking towards the street; (3) the verbal direction of, "Stop", (4) the actor stopped in front of the foam mat; (5) the verbal praise, "Good stopping;" and (6) the actor walking back up the driveway and continuing to play.

## Viewing the video

The video was burned onto a DVD and given to Bryce's mother during one of his home visits. It was decided that Bryce would watch the video and then immediately practice remaining safe in his front yard, while his younger brother took his morning nap. His mother was committed to showing him the video and practicing this skill at least three times each week. The video was shown to Bryce on a large television located in his family room. Due to his current needs, this room was very bare, which provided him with a distraction-free viewing environment. He sat on his mother's lap as the video played. In order to keep him calm and engaged, she provided sensory input to his body (e.g., rubbing his legs and squeezing his hands). This added input helped him to remain seated with his eyes on the television screen for the duration of the video.

## Facilitating skill development following the video

As a way to proactively manage Bryce's behaviors outside, his mother was instructed to model the play strategies shown in the video. His teacher hoped that as Bryce was able to remain engaged in appropriate outdoor play for longer periods of time, the number of times that he would try to run into the street would decrease. His mother was also instructed to stay close to him as he approached the end of the driveway so that she could help him to stop as he reached the foam mats. Bryce was praised for his ability to stop at the end of the driveway, whether he did it on his own or was provided with physical support.

## Child outcomes

Bryce and his mother were observed while playing outside two weeks later. His mother reported that he had watched the video and practiced the skill seven times since the initial viewing. During a 15-minute observation, Bryce only approached the end of the driveway four times. On three of these instances, Bryce stopped and said, "Stop," as he reached the foam mats at the end of the driveway. On the last instance, Bryce was walking quickly toward the end of the driveway, which made his mother nervous. She yelled, "Stop!" from over ten feet away and he immediately stopped. He quickly looked back toward his mother in anticipation of her cheering. Bryce's mother was thrilled with his progress and was excited to have a new environment that she and her boys could play in together.

### Fading and generalization

The use of this video was faded over time. The use of the visual stopping point at the end of the driveway continued to be used. Like all two-year-olds, Bryce continued to need occasional reminders to stay on the driveway. However, his mother was very comfortable managing both him and his younger brother during outdoor play.

## GRETA (TWO-AND-A-HALF YEARS OLD): SWIMMING LESSONS
### Child background

Greta, a two-and-a-half-year-old girl with a medical diagnosis of ASD, was receiving weekly in-home services through her local school district. Greta loved to swim in her neighborhood pool. Her parents enrolled her in a parent and child swimming class in the hope of increasing her swimming skills and to provide her with some special one-on-one time with her mother. Greta was familiar with the swimming school where the lessons were held as she often sat with her mother and watched as her older sister took a class. Her parents felt as though swimming lessons would be a good match for her current abilities. She was able to follow one-step directions (e.g., "Kick feet") and was beginning to use two-word phrases to make requests and to comment on the things that she saw. She enjoyed interacting with other people, although her interactions were not always appropriate. For example, she would initiate interactions with another child by poking her face or by repetitively engaging in a familiar routine of chase while saying, "Gonna get you!" Her interaction skills were best when toys were not present and when engaged in a gross motor/sensory activity (e.g., swinging, jumping). Her parents also thought that the structure and consistency provided by this swimming school would provide Greta with a greater chance of success. On the first day of class, Greta began crying as soon as they entered the pool. Her mother attempted to calm her down by singing her favorite songs, doing silly things with the pool toys, and giving her big hugs. Nothing seemed to work and after about 15 minutes they got out of the pool. The second day of class was not any better. This time, Greta's mother kept her in the pool for 20 minutes before finally giving up and leaving. Greta's parents were surprised by her behavior as she loved to swim and was familiar with the environment. They also felt as though they had done a good job of preparing her for the lessons by using some of the swimming school's terminology during bath time, engaging in frequent discussions about the things that would happen at swim school, and observing her sister's swimming class.

## Description of the video

A BVM video was made for Greta to decrease her fears and increase her enjoyment during her swimming lesson. Greta's early intervention teacher asked her mother to record a few short clips of Greta's older sister at the swimming school, including one of her getting into the pool, one of her having fun in the pool, and one of her getting out of the pool. Her mother chose to record the footage using her smartphone. In order to eliminate the need for editing, Greta's mother had been asked to say three different phrases into the camera while filming specific behaviors. As Greta's sister stepped into the pool, her mother said, "Time for swimming." While Greta's sister was swimming, her mother said, "Swimming is fun!" As Greta's sister stepped out of the pool, her mother said, "All done swimming." The combined length of the three videos was less than two minutes.

## Viewing the video

The three video clips were shown to Greta on her mother's smartphone. The videos were not combined together through video editing and instead were shown to Greta in succession without interruption (i.e., the first video was shown, immediately followed by the second and then the third). Once the videos were recorded, there were four more days until Greta's next swimming lesson. Due to the severity of her negative reaction to swimming class, it was decided that Greta should watch the videos every day. On the day of her next swimming lesson, Greta's mother showed her the videos in the car before going into the swimming school. The car provided Greta with the opportunity to watch the videos in a quiet and minimally distracting environment that would have been very difficult to achieve within the swimming school.

## Facilitating skill development following the video

During class, Greta's mother used the same language that she used in the video including, "Time for swimming," "Swimming is fun!," and "All done swimming." If needed, she was told to follow through with the calm-down sequence that was modeled at their last home visit. The calm-down sequence consisted of the following: holding Greta and rocking side-to-side while singing the ABC's, and then giving ten big squeezes while slowly counting to ten. Greta and her mother had been practicing this sequence over the previous few days while she was calm so she was familiar with it and could anticipate what would happen next.

## Child outcomes

After watching the videos four times, Greta calmly entered the pool and remained calm for the duration of her third lesson. Greta and her mother completed the calm-down routine two times throughout the lesson to proactively manage her behaviors.

## Fading and generalization

The sequence of videos was shown each day following her third lesson and only a few times upon request following her fourth lesson (approximately 15 times in total). After her fifth lesson, Greta no longer needed the videos. Greta continued to remain calm during her swimming lessons and both she and her mother looked forward to swimming school each week.

# RUDY (THREE YEARS OLD): IMITATING MOTOR MOVEMENTS

## Child background

Rudy, a three-year-old boy with a medical diagnosis of ASD, had been receiving a combination of in-home and center-based services through his local school district since he was 20 months old. The amount of services provided to Rudy and his family increased over time in order to meet their growing needs. The size of his educational team grew as well, and soon consisted of his parents, special education teacher, a speech and language pathologist, an occupational therapist, and an autism specialist. Rudy's development in all areas was significantly delayed. At just under three years old, Rudy's team was still working on increasing his ability to imitate the motor movements of an adult (e.g., clapping hands, putting both arms up in the air), skills that typically begin to develop between 10 and 18 months of age (Jones 2007).[1] The ability to imitate another person's actions is a pivotal skill in early development as it is one of the core building blocks to a variety of later developing language and play skills. Rudy's ability to shift his attention toward an adult in order to share enjoyment or to observe the adult's actions was increasing nicely. However, his educational team (including his parents) was frustrated with his lack of progress in the area of imitation and was ready to try a new way to teach this skill.

---

1 Jones' findings regarding the age at which imitation skills begin to develop contradicts a widely agreed upon notion that many infants have the ability to imitate tongue protrusion, mouth opening, and lip protrusion as early as 12 to 21 days old (Meltzoff and Moore 1977). The results of Jones' research indicated that infants first learn to imitate actions that act as auditory cues for subsequent behaviors (i.e., tapping a table with a toy, opening mouth saying, "Ahh") between 8 and 12 months of age. Jones reported that between 10 and 12 months of age, infants are able to imitate familiar behaviors that are often facilitated and rewarded by parents (i.e., clapping hands, waving). It wasn't until 16 to 18 months of age that Jones found infants to imitate actions that are not cued by sound and are invisible to the infant (i.e., hand on head, tongue protrusion).

## Description of the video

A BVM video was created to teach Rudy how to imitate the actions that go along with the song, "If You're Happy and You Know It." These actions included clapping hands, stomping feet, patting knees, and putting both arms up in the air. The actors in the video included Rudy's early childhood special education teacher and four young children including three girls and one boy. The child actors were chosen based on their availability and their ability to follow simple directions involving motor movements. Each child actor was filmed demonstrating all of the targeted actions. Rudy's teacher was filmed giving a simple direction related to the action (e.g., "Clap hands," or "Do this") and then modeling the action. Filming took place in a variety of locations. The only consistent element of each clip was that each actor sat on a chair in front of a solid colored wall (or door if no solid colored wall was available). The raw video footage was edited to display the following sequence: (1) Rudy's teacher clapping hands while saying, "Clap hands;" (2) the first child actor clapping hands; (3) Rudy's teacher clapping hands while saying, "Do this;" (4) the second child actor clapping hands; (5) Rudy's teacher clapping hands while saying, "Clap hands;" and (6) the third child actor clapping hands. This same sequence was repeated for each of the remaining actions. Rudy's teacher thought that Rudy would be more successful imitating actions when paired with a verbal direction. She planned to fade the use of the verbal prompts as he began to imitate the actions.

## Viewing the video

Rudy watched the video two times each week, once during one of his in-center therapy sessions and once during one of his weekly home visits. He was immediately given the opportunity to imitate the actions following each viewing. Rudy watched the video using various different pieces of equipment including a hand-held DVD player and a laptop within his home and a desktop computer and interactive whiteboard within his classroom. His mother was given a copy of the video to use on the remaining five days of each week.

Due to a variety of family circumstances, it was difficult for Rudy's mother to show him the video more than once each week. Many weeks went by in which his mother did not show him the video at all.

## Facilitating skill development following the video

Prior to video modeling, Rudy's educational team was using discrete trial training, a method derived from the basic principles of applied behavior analysis, in order to increase his imitation skills. They continued to target his ability to imitate actions following the viewing using this strategy. For example, immediately following the viewing, Rudy sat across from his teacher at a child-sized table. Another adult sat directly behind Rudy in order to provide him with physical prompts. Each discrete trial consisted of the following steps: (1) Rudy's teacher said, "Clap hands" or "Do this" while clapping her hands; (2) Rudy was given a two to three second period of time in which to imitate the action; (3) if Rudy didn't clap his hands, the adult sitting behind him would provide him with a physical prompt in order to help him to clap his hands; and (4) Rudy was given specific verbal praise ("Good clapping hands!") and was allowed to watch a small spinning and light-up toy for five to ten seconds. The adult who sat behind Rudy was instructed to follow the system of least prompts. For example, if Rudy did not respond to a light tap on the back of his arms, the adult was asked to push his arms forward a few inches before finally taking his hands and making them clap. After five to eight trials with each action, Rudy's teacher brought the activity to a closure by singing, "If You're Happy and You Know It" while modeling the actions one final time.

## Child outcomes

Rudy's ability to imitate actions continued to increase very slowly over time; however, his educational team did not feel as though his progress was directly related to BVM. Rudy's teacher felt as though he would have made more significant progress if given the opportunity to watch the video and practice the skills more than twice each week.

# PRESCHOOL CLASSROOM (THREE TO FIVE YEARS OLD): CLASSROOM ROUTINES
## Background

BVM videos depicting a variety of classroom routines were created to help preschoolers function more independently in various different classroom settings. These videos were developed to benefit all children ages three to five who participated in programs within our school district's early childhood building. There were three different programs serving young children that were housed in this one center, including a preschool program offering half-day programming options, a childcare program offering all-day childcare and an early childhood special education program. Most of the children who were receiving special education services were also enrolled in the preschool program and/or the childcare program. Within these programs there were many different teachers, all teaching the classroom routines in very different ways. Some of the teachers used pictures to demonstrate the expected behaviors while some relied primarily on verbal instruction to teach the routines. Some of the teachers didn't specifically teach the behaviors needed to successfully complete these routines, but hoped that the children would learn them through observation and repetition. The teachers' expectations of their students during these routines were as inconsistent as the way in which they taught them. For example, some teachers were comfortable with their students making a comment during circle time; however, other teachers wanted their students to raise their hands if they had something to say. As special education teachers, we found this lack of consistency confusing for students with special needs as well as for the students who participated in up to three different classrooms and/or programs throughout their school week. In order to benefit all of the students, not just those receiving special education services, we felt it would be helpful to directly teach the classroom routines in a more systematic, visual manner. We decided to create BVM videos to teach the following routines: lining up, walking down the hall, washing hands, cleaning up after snacks, circle time, tidying toys in a classroom, tidying toys in the gym, and completing a calm-down routine.

## Description of the lining up and walking down the hall video

A BVM video was created to teach the children how to appropriately line up at the door with their peers before transitioning out of the classroom as a group as well as how to appropriately walk down the hall. Prior to creating the video, a task analysis of the routine was completed to identify the various steps within the routine. We decided that it was important for the video to address the skills of lining up with appropriate body space and knowing what to do with your hands while in line. We recruited several parents who agreed to bring their children to the school on a non-school day to be filmed for the video. The children ranged in age from four to seven years. Some had special needs and some did not. Before filming the routine, we taught the specific skills within the routine to the children. This video required editing and voice-over narration in order to highlight the specific expectations of this routine.

In the beginning of this video, the words "Lining up" appear on-screen while the off-screen narrator states the title. The teacher is shown standing at the door. She calls out to the children, "Okay friends, time to line up at the door." The children then walk slowly to the door. The off-screen narrator states, "The teacher said it's time to line up at the door. All of the kids are using their walking feet to line up at the door." On-screen, the children are shown walking to the door and lining up single file using appropriate body space. The narrator then states, "Look, Liv is walking to the end of the line," while Liv is shown walking to the end of the line. The narrator then states, "When you're standing in line, you need to keep your hands on your own body." This beginning section was filmed in one errorless take. It was later edited to take out any background noise and to add narration. The video then shows still shots of what the children can choose to do with their hands while they wait in line. These options include keeping their hands down at their sides, in their pockets, folded together in front of them, or on their hips. While the still shots are shown on-screen, the narrator describes these options. The children are then shown standing in line with good body space with their hands in appropriate positions. The narrator then states, "The kids are standing in line with their hands on their own bodies. Good job." The narrator then says, "Walking down the hall" while those words appear onscreen. The narrator states, "The teacher will tell you when it's time to walk. You can start to walk when the person in front of you starts to walk." The children are then shown walking single file behind the teacher out the door and down the hallway. During editing, the background noise was removed, background music was added, and a voice-over was added, "Remember, use walking feet and keep your hands on your own body. The end." The resulting video is about one-and-a-half minutes long.

## Description of the circle time video

A BVM video was created to teach the children the skills of how to appropriately participate in the circle time routine. Prior to filming, a task analysis was completed to determine the important skills to be highlighted in the video. The skills determined to be salient to the circle time routine included: (1) finding a designated place to sit; (2) sitting cross-legged on the floor; (3) keeping hands in lap; (4) using listening ears; (5) keeping eyes on the teacher; and (6) keeping a quiet mouth. The same group of children used to create the lining up video was used to make this video. These children were taught the required skills before filming began. However, we knew that since editing and voice-over narration was required, we would be able to provide verbal directions to the children during filming, if needed.

At the beginning of the completed video, the teacher says, "Boys and girls, time for circle time." The students then slowly walk over to sit on a carpet square in the circle time area. This sequence was edited with a voice-over stating, "The teacher said it was circle time. The boys and girls are walking over to find a place to sit. Your teacher will tell you where to sit. It might be on a carpet square or it might be something different." This statement was added because not all teachers within the building have the children sit on a carpet square. Some have their students sit on other things such as a piece of tape, a shape on a large rug, or a name tag. The video then shows the children finding a place to sit and sitting cross-legged with their hands in their laps. At this point in the video, the teacher begins to read a book to the class. The voice-over narration then continues to highlight the circle time rules. As each rule is mentioned, a still photo of a child following that rule is shown in order to demonstrate the skill to the viewer. The remaining video narration is as follows, "The kids look like they're ready for circle time to start... The kids are keeping their eyes on the teacher... The kids are keeping their hands in their laps... The kids are sitting cross-legged... The kids are using their listening ears... The kids are keeping their mouths quiet... Everyone is following the circle time rules. Good job friends." All video clips were muted and a quiet and soothing song was added into the background of the entire video.

## Description of the calm-down video

A BVM video was created to teach the skill of walking to the calm-down corner and completing a specific calm-down routine when a child is upset. The teachers within the building were asked to create a calm-down corner for the children to access as needed within each of their classrooms. The calm-down corner consisted of a small table and chair with three tubs. Each tub contained an object for one calming activity. A number strip (including the numerals one through ten) and a picture of the teacher using the calming object was posted on the outside of the tub. We chose activities for each tub that the child would be able to complete independently and that the child could complete at home even if the objects weren't present. The first tub contained a small, firm ball that the child would squeeze ten times. The second tub contained a rolling pin that the child would roll over her thighs ten times. The third tub contained a large rubber band that the child would grasp with both hands and pull apart while taking ten deep breaths. A feather was hung from the handle of the tub so the child would know that she was taking productive breaths. The child could watch the feather move as she exhaled through her mouth. Our hope was that when a child was upset, she could sit down at the table and complete the sequence of three calming activities in order to calm down. Please see Figure 1.2 for an example of a calm-down corner.

*Figure 1.2. A calm-down corner*

For this video, a four-year-old girl, Evie, was filmed completing the calm-down routine. Prior to filming, Evie was taught the routine; however, we knew that any on-screen instructions that were needed could be edited out. The video begins with a still shot of Evie with an angry look on her face and her arms crossed. Voice-over narration was added stating, "Evie, I see that you're having a hard time right now. Why don't you go over to the calm-down corner to make your body feel better?" The video then shows Evie walking over to sit at the small table with the three tubs of calming toys. She pulls the first tub toward her, takes the ball out of the tub, and squeezes it while counting out loud to ten. She replaces the toy and proceeds to the next tub. She pulls the second tub toward her, takes the rolling pin out of the tub, and rolls it on each leg while counting out loud to ten. She puts the rolling pin back and moves onto the third tub. She then pulls the third tub toward her, takes the band out of the tub and takes ten deep breaths while pulling the rubber band and exhaling toward the feather. She replaces the rubber band and puts the tub back in its place. During filming, Evie needed a few verbal instructions in order to complete the routine. These instructions were later edited out. The sound of Evie counting and her deep breaths remained in the video, and calming background music was added during all transitions such as when Evie put away one object and moved onto the next tub. The video ends with a still shot of Evie looking calm and happy with voice-over narration stating, "Good job in the calm-down corner. Your body looks just right."

## Viewing the videos

The classroom-routine BVM videos were burned onto DVDs and distributed to every teacher within the building prior to the first day of class in the fall. The teachers were instructed to show the videos to the whole class on the large interactive white board mounted on the classroom wall prior to each routine. It was recommended that the videos be shown daily for the first few weeks of school and then faded from use as the children learned the routines.

## Child outcomes

The use of these videos was not mandatory so the implementation varied widely throughout the building. Some teachers showed each video daily prior to the routine for several weeks at the beginning of the school year, while some of the teachers didn't show any of the videos at all. The teachers who used the videos reported high rates of success including calmer transitions between routine activities and greater participation and independence during routines. Several teachers reported that they noticed a decrease in student anxiety during these routines. By watching the videos, the children were able to learn what was expected of them within each routine and were able to participate with greater comfort and reduced anxiety. Many of the teachers who did not initially use the videos within their classrooms later decided to begin showing them to their students due to these high rates of success.

## Fading and generalization

Most of the teachers began fading the use of these videos after about two weeks of school. However, they often brought them back after an extended break from school such as the winter break or as a general refresher. For students with special needs, these videos were typically faded over a longer period. The videos were then shown to the student individually on a laptop computer in the classroom prior to the routine.

# 2

# VIDEO SELF-MODELING (VSM)

Video Self-Modeling (VSM) differs from Basic Video Modeling (BVM) in one fundamental way: the main actor in a VSM video is always the learner himself. While BVM involves the learner watching a video of another person demonstrating a skill, VSM involves the learner watching a video of himself successfully demonstrating the target skill or routine. Watching a video of oneself appropriately demonstrating the expected behaviors not only teaches the learner what he needs to do, but it also increases his confidence in his own ability to do it! The learner is then able to imitate these self-modeled behaviors to successfully demonstrate the targeted skill.

In his years of research, Albert Bandura (1977) determined that modeling is a powerful way to learn and refine skills. He found that in order for a child to imitate others, the child must be able to attend to the model and must be motivated to do so. Bandura also reported that a child is more motivated to attend to a model that is "competent" and similar to the child in physical characteristics, gender, and age. Therefore, having the child view himself doing the modeling has the potential to cause the greatest change. What better model than the learner watching himself performing at his best?

While we discussed the ages of children who benefit from video modeling in the introduction of this book, it is important to look at this again in reference to VSM. The reason to take a second look is that in order for VSM to be effective, the child must recognize himself in the video. If he is not able to identify himself, the benefits of having the child act as his own model will be lost on him. So what is the youngest age at which VSM is effective? Research shows that self-recognition occurs in children between 18 to 24 months (Lewis and Brooks-Gunn 1979). It is important to note that this research was conducted on typically developing children and that this skill may or may not emerge at a later time in children with autism spectrum disorders (ASD). One way to test if the child is able to recognize himself is to draw a dot with a marker on his nose and then have him look in the mirror. If he reaches for his own nose while looking in the mirror, he recognizes that the image in the mirror is himself. You can also have the child look at photos of himself to see if he is able to identify himself. Buggey (2009) conducted an informal self-recognition study on children between the ages of birth and three. He had young children watch themselves live on the screen of a video camera that he had turned to face the child. None of the children under the age of one seemed to recognize themselves on-screen. One child between the ages of one and two recognized himself on-screen. Almost all of the children between the ages of two and three recognized themselves on-screen. In this informal study, Buggey noted that there did not seem to be a difference in the self-recognition skills of children with and without developmental delays. How ASD affects a child's ability to recognize himself on-screen is an area that needs further research. The simple answer to our question seems to be two years; this will inevitably vary, however, depending upon the individual.

Peter Dowrick is often referred to as the "father" of VSM and has been experimenting with and using this strategy for more than 30 years. According to Dowrick, there are two different kinds of VSM videos, Positive Self-Review and Feedforward (Dowrick 1999). In Positive Self-Review videos, the goal is to increase the frequency of a behavior that is already in the learner's repertoire. For example, if the learner already knows how to raise his hand at circle time but doesn't do it consistently, you could create a video of him raising his hand every time before speaking. These types of videos typically require little editing to remove verbal or physical prompts from the raw footage. Because the learner can already demonstrate the behavior, no verbal or physical prompts are required to elicit the behavior. However, it can sometimes be difficult to obtain enough raw footage that depicts the target behavior if it is an extremely low-frequency behavior. Feedforward is the other type of VSM. With Feedforward videos, the learner views himself demonstrating a skill that is slightly beyond his current capabilities. These types of videos can be used in several different scenarios: (1) if the learner is able to demonstrate some but not all behaviors necessary to perform the target skill; (2) if the learner is only able to perform the skill at a low level of mastery; or (3) if the learner needs support to demonstrate the behaviors necessary to perform the skill. For example, if a learner is unable to raise his hand before speaking without adult support, you could create a video that depicts the learner independently raising his hand. In creating the video, the learner would be prompted by an adult to raise his hand and the prompt would be removed during the editing process. Feedforward VSM videos typically require more editing than Positive Self-Review VSM videos in order to remove prompts.

VSM videos can be used to teach a wide variety of skills. As noted above, VSM videos are most effective at increasing the frequency of a behavior that is demonstrated infrequently, shaping and refining existing behaviors, and teaching new behaviors, all of which increases the learner's independence in demonstrating a skill or routine. More specifically, we have used VSM videos with young children to reduce anxiety, increase independence in home and school routines, increase social skills, and decrease unexpected behaviors. One added benefit of recording the learner demonstrating the targeted skill or routine is what is sometimes called the "movie star" effect. Many children increase their ability to demonstrate the expected behaviors during the act of filming the skill or routine just because they know they are being recorded! This makes for better raw footage, meaning less time editing, as well as a jump-start on intervention.

# STEPS TO VIDEO SELF-MODELING

We have identified ten steps that we feel are important to follow when creating and using VSM with young children with ASD. These steps are described in detail below. Many of these steps are similar to those followed when creating BVM videos, but some of the steps are specific to VSM.

## Step One: Identify a skill or routine that you would like to target

In identifying a skill or routine that you would like to target in a VSM video, it is important to remember that the child will be the actor. The target skill or routine needs to be something that the child has some capacity to demonstrate, either inconsistently or with prompting.

## Step Two: Identify and assemble the materials needed

Creating your VSM video will go more smoothly and efficiently if you first take the time to identify and assemble all of the materials needed. The first thing to plan for is the presence of your main actor, the child. If you are creating a video in which the child will need prompting or support to complete the skill or routine, you may also need two adults, one to hold the camera and one to prompt the child. If the skill you are targeting is relatively stationary, you may be able to use a tripod in place of the second adult. Depending on the skill or routine you are targeting and the child's level of independence, you may be able to get the needed raw footage without an additional adult to provide support; just plan ahead. You may also need to gather or create any necessary visual supports. For example, if you are targeting a self-help routine such as dressing or brushing teeth, does the child need pictures representing the steps to be successful?

To get the raw footage used to create a VSM video, you will need a video-recording device. You will also need editing software, as almost all VSM videos require editing. You may find that just the act of recording the child encourages him to demonstrate more of the expected behaviors than he is typically able to demonstrate because of the "movie star" effect mentioned earlier. For example, if you tell the child that you are making a movie of him raising his hand before he speaks, he may remember to raise his hand while you are filming. In this case, you might not need to edit the raw footage video at all. In general, however, you will probably need to edit most VSM videos. Many video-recording devices come with built-in editing software and most computer software bundles come with video-editing software such as Windows Movie Maker (PC) or iMovie (Mac).

When you are assembling materials for filming, don't forget to include the items that the child will use in the video (e.g., toys, self-help items). It is also a good idea to think about how you plan to show the video to the child. How and where you show the video will determine what items you will need for playback. The current options for playing back a video include a television, computer, portable DVD player, interactive whiteboard, electronic tablet, smartphone, or the actual video-recording device. Depending on how you play the video for the child, you may also need a DVD or a USB flash drive.

## Step Three: Complete a task analysis of the skill or routine and collect baseline data

We find it helpful to complete a task analysis of the skill or routine as well as to collect baseline data prior to creating and using the video. As noted in Chapter 1, "task analysis" sounds scary but it actually just involves deconstructing the skill or routine to identify its smallest elements (all expected behaviors). Before you create the video or begin trying to make changes to the child's behavior, it is a good idea to collect baseline data. This simply means observing the child to see what he is currently able to do. Since the child will be the actor in the video, it is essential that you know exactly what he is able to do and what level of support he needs.

## Step Four: Make a plan for the filming of the video

We recommend thorough planning before you begin the filming process. You will first need to decide which type of modeling video to create. See Appendix A for more information on how to choose the type of video modeling that best matches the child and the target skill. Once you have determined the type of video you want to create, we suggest you write an outline that includes everything you want included in the video. Since the child will be the actor, you will not be able to write a prescribed script as you would with BVM or Point-of-view Video Modeling (PVM) videos. However, it is important for you and any other people involved (other actors or support people) to know what the plan is for the video and what your expectations are. For example, in a video created to increase the child's ability to respond to a peer's request to play, the peer actor will need to know what to say to the child (e.g., "Want to play in the kitchen?"). In a video created to increase the child's independence in completing a self-help routine, the adult who is prompting the child will need to know how much and what kind of support (verbal, visual, or physical) to give the child as well as when to back out of the camera focus area. The person holding the camera will need to know where to focus the camera in order to film the important actions and to make sure to get shots that don't include the adult support person.

## Step Five: Record the video

It's time to start filming! How you proceed in recording raw footage for your VSM video will depend on which type of VSM video you are creating, a Positive Self-Review or a Feedforward video. Remember, in a Positive Self-Review video you are trying to increase the frequency of an expected behavior that the child already demonstrates. The challenge in getting raw footage for this type of video is in setting up the environment to best elicit the target behavior. You can either record the child in a naturally occurring situation or you can set up an artificial or prompted scenario. In the situation explained earlier of increasing the behavior of the child raising his hand before he speaks, you could get the raw footage in one of two ways. You could record the duration of a circle time hoping that the child will raise his hand before speaking, or you could have someone prompt the child to raise his hand and later remove the prompt from the raw footage.

Remember, in Feedforward videos you are recording the child demonstrating a skill that is slightly beyond his current capabilities. In filming the raw footage for these videos, as noted earlier, you will probably need a second person to help prompt the child through the steps of the skill that he is not yet able to complete independently. There are three different types of prompts: verbal, visual (e.g., pointing, pictures), and physical. When recording the footage for your video, you will have to plan for how you will remove these prompts from the final video. During the editing process, you will be able to mute any verbal prompts. If possible, you may want to give visual prompts such as pointing out of the focus of the camera or have the person giving the visual prompt quickly step out of the camera focus area. You will need to remove all physical prompts from the footage so make sure you have enough raw footage of the child performing the behavior independently after the person giving the physical prompt has stepped out of the camera focus area. For example, if you are creating a video to help the child learn to unzip his jacket, the person giving a physical prompt could help the child begin unzipping and then step out of the camera focus area to allow you to get footage of the child independently unzipping his jacket. This assumes that the child has the skills to keep unzipping once he is given help to get started. Remember, Feedforward videos should teach skills that are just slightly beyond the child's current capabilities. If the skill is too far beyond his reach, a video will not be effective.

## Step Six: Edit the video footage

In this step, you will learn how to create a VSM video from your raw footage. As noted in Step Two, before beginning the filming process you will need to identify how you will edit your raw footage. If you are using the built-in editing software on your video-recording device, you will be given the option to download this software onto your computer when you plug the camera into the computer. Some cameras allow the user to edit footage directly on the camera. Other editing options include using computer software such as Windows Movie Maker (PC) or iMovie (Mac).

As with all things, it may take a little practice to get the hang of video editing. The amount of time it takes for you to edit raw footage into a VSM video will decrease as you get more familiar with the editing software and with the process in general. As noted in Chapter 1, do not fall into the trap of thinking that your video needs to be perfect. The child will not notice little flaws. Also, the amount of time you put into making the video "perfect" may not necessarily pay off in the end. A less sophisticated VSM video can be just as effective as a professional-looking VSM video. So, have fun editing and remember that you will get faster with more experience.

As mentioned in Chapter 1, the editing process will be similar no matter what software you choose to use. Below are eight steps that can be followed when editing your VSM video. It is not imperative that all of these steps be completed and you may find that editing is easier when some of these steps are completed in a different order. While most of these steps are similar to the editing steps described in the previous chapter, there are some components that are specific to creating VSM videos.

1.  Import the raw footage into the editing software. There are several ways to accomplish this and it will vary depending on your software.

2.  Splice the raw footage to include only the parts that you want in the final video. Remember, you can mute any unwanted sounds and prompts such as off-screen directions to the actors and distracting background noises, so you don't necessarily have to discard these parts. Depending on the purpose of your video, you will probably want to remove any clips that show physical or visual prompts.

3.  You will need to decide if you want to use any still shots within the video. Still shots are a powerful tool frequently used in BVM videos to highlight a skill; however, we do not typically use still shots in VSM videos. We prefer to depict the skill or routine in its entirety at its normal pace to provide a clear example of the target skill.

4.  Mute any unwanted sounds. Undesirable sounds may include distracting background noises and off-screen prompts.

5.  Add voice-over narration, if desired. Narration is useful in highlighting specific steps, rules or expectations in BVM videos. As with still shots, we do not typically add narration to VSM videos. Because we are teaching independence or increasing the fluency or performance level of an existing skill, we find that it is more beneficial to simply provide a visual depiction of the skill or routine. Adding voice-over narration may add a level of prompting that will need to be faded later in time. However, you may want to add voice to the title page to identify the skill or routine such as, "Lucas raises his hand at circle time!"

6.  Add background music. Music is a powerful element in a VSM video. It can be used to demonstrate that the targeted skill or behavior is an enjoyable activity and can also increase the viewer's enjoyment while watching the video, therefore, increasing the likelihood that he will attend to the entire video. Remember to match the tone and pace of the music to the activity in the video. We suggest instrumental music for most videos so the words of the song do not interfere with the message of the video. There are many websites that offer free music and sounds that can be downloaded for use in videos (e.g., Freeplaymusic.com and Beemp3.com).

7.  At the end of the video, make sure to add specific verbal praise for successful on-screen demonstration of the targeted skill or behavior such as, "Good job raising your hand!" This would be the one place in the video that you could add a still shot of the child. It can also be motivating to add

a video or audio clip of a reinforcer at the end of the video. For example, an audio clip of applause or kids saying, "Yay," can be very reinforcing for a young learner.

8. Save the video for playback. As mentioned earlier, how you save your finished video will depend on how you plan to show it to the child.

## Step Seven: Show the video to the child

Compared to the editing process, showing the video to the child is a breeze. Depending on where you plan to show the video, there are many options for video playback. These options include a television, computer, portable DVD player, interactive whiteboard, electronic tablet, smartphone, etc. In order for the video to be as effective as possible, it is important to give the child the opportunity to watch the video in its entirety without interruption. According to Buggey, "One of the strengths of VSM—especially with children with autism—is that no social obligations are present" (2009, p.73). If the adult is interjecting and making comments to the child during the viewing, it is no longer an individual activity. It places demands on the child to respond, which has the potential to cause some unexpected behaviors. An interruption-free viewing environment is sometimes easier to accomplish in the child's home. If the child is watching the video at school, it might be best to play it on a portable device in a quiet area of the classroom or in the hall. You can also try to see if the child will tolerate wearing headphones.

Every child is different and may benefit from different frequencies of viewing. Some children may need to watch the video every day, while others may demonstrate progress when only given a few opportunities to watch the video each week. While we have found that viewing the video immediately prior to practicing the skill or routine makes for an easy transition, it is not necessary.

## Step Eight: Facilitate skill development following the viewing of the video

VSM is not a stand-alone intervention. In one of Dowrick's earliest studies that examined the effects of VSM on the swimming abilities of children with spina bifida, he explained the importance of continued skill facilitation through recurrent swimming lessons (1980). Just as it would be harmful to place a child in a pool without adult support after merely viewing a VSM video of himself swimming independently, it would be impractical to discontinue all additional strategies and supports when targeting any other skill or routine. While a child can sometimes respond immediately to VSM (making it seem like a quick-fix intervention), in most cases you should continue facilitating the child's skills using other time-honored teaching strategies.

## Step Nine: Monitor the child's progress to determine if changes need to be made

In this step of the VSM process, you will want to determine if the child has made progress since the VSM video was introduced. In order to do this, you will want to record data on the child's ability to demonstrate the targeted expected behaviors. You will then have solid evidence that the child is or is not making sufficient progress. "Taking data" may sound difficult, but it simply means watching the child complete the skill or routine and taking notes on what the child is able to do. Sample data sheets are available for use in Appendix C.

## Step Ten: Problem solve if progress is slow

Is the child making less progress than you had hoped? There are many things to consider if this is the case. Here are a few questions you can ask yourself when trying to identify a reason for slow progress.

- Are you showing the video often enough?

- Is there a better time within the child's day that the video could be shown?

- Is the environment in which the child is watching the video too distracting?

- Is the video too long?

- Would a different type of video modeling (PVM or VSM) be better for this skill or for the child?

- Does the skill or routine that you are targeting include too many steps or are the expected behaviors too far out of the child's reach?

Remember, it is important to make only one change at a time or it may be difficult to figure out which change made the biggest impact. The knowledge you gain in problem solving why a VSM video was not as effective as you had hoped will be useful information when creating subsequent videos.

## VIDEO SELF-MODELING CASE STUDIES

We have included the following five case studies as examples to demonstrate how we have used VSM with the families and children with whom we work. The studies focus on a variety of skills and routines at home, school, and in the community. The studies are arranged in order by the age of the child, from 22 months to 6 years.

## BRIG (22 MONTHS OLD):
## GETTING DRESSED
### Child background

Brig, a 22-month-old girl, began receiving early intervention services at the age of 20 months under the educational category of ASD. At the time of her initial evaluation, it was reported that Brig had lost the eight words she had previously mastered and was now only able to occasionally imitate the sign for "More." Brig's parents were masters at anticipating her needs, which really minimized her need to communicate. She liked the way that certain sensory activities made her body feel and so she was observed to frequently melt into her parents' arms for big hugs, run and crash into pillows, rock forward and back while seated, and roll around in piles of blankets. Her eye contact was minimal, but it was best during these activities. Brig enjoyed playing with toys, but she didn't always play with them as they were meant to be played with. Although she was more focused on objects than her neurotypical peers, Brig was often able to shift her attention toward others during play with toys in order to observe and imitate their actions. Brig was happiest while she was watching her favorite videos on the family room television. Brig had a difficult time participating in many daily routines. She displayed many inappropriate behaviors such as crying, running away, dropping to the floor, or throwing objects when expected to eat at the table, lay down for a nap in her crib, put on socks and shoes before leaving the house, and go upstairs for a diaper change. Brig's parents reported that their number one priority was for Brig to cooperate more during everyday routines. Their hope was to first target her level of cooperation during these routines and then to target a variety of other skills including communication and increased independence.

## Description of the video

A VSM video was created to increase Brig's cooperation during the dressing routine. On a regularly scheduled home visit, Brig was filmed while getting dressed with her grandmother. Brig's early intervention teacher was the person recording this routine. During filming, Brig's grandmother followed through with the previously discussed routine, which included the following steps: (1) change diaper; (2) massage each leg with lotion while slowly counting to ten out loud; (3) put pants on; (4) massage each arm with lotion while slowly counting to ten out loud; (5) put shirt on; and (6) big cheers for Brig! The filming started once Brig's clean diaper was on. Steps 2 and 4 were added because massage was another sensory activity that Brig enjoyed and this instantly calmed her down. The filming process took less than five minutes. During the editing process, all of the background noise (except for the big cheers at the end) was muted because Brig was crying in most of the raw footage. A slow and very calming instrumental song was added to the background of the entire video. The following voice-over narration was added to coordinate with the actions in the video: "Time for lotion," "Pants on," "Pull pants up," "More lotion," "Here's your shirt," "On your head," "One arm in," and "Two arms in." Additional narration (slowly counting to ten) was added during the massages with lotion. A title page was added to the beginning of the video with the following text and voice-over narration, "Brig gets dressed!" Closing text was added to the end of the video with the following text and voice-over narration, "The end." The completed video was three minutes. The video was saved onto a USB flash drive and then saved onto her mother's laptop.

## Viewing the video

Because the transition up to her bedroom was difficult for Brig, her family decided that it would be best to show her the video in her room. They thought that she would be more willing to go upstairs to "watch a movie" than she would be to "get dressed." While watching the video, Brig sat on an adult's lap and the laptop sat on Brig's lap. Brig watched the video three mornings each week. It was suggested by her early intervention teacher that she watch the video more often to start off with (at least four or five times each week); however, this was not manageable for her family as they had other children to care for. Brig enjoyed watching the video and remained quiet and still in the adult's lap. She often smiled at the end of the video when her grandmother cheered!

## Facilitating skill development following the video

Brig's grandmother was typically the person facilitating Brig's skills during the dressing routine following the video. Her grandmother followed through with the routine in the same way it was demonstrated in the video, and she continued to follow through with most of the strategies discussed during weekly home visits. These strategies included the following: set up the environment prior to initiating the routine; start and end the routine in the same way each day; limit use of language to one, two and three-word phrases (especially when she is upset); use exaggerated gestures and facial expressions so Brig checks in with her grandmother more often; add in pauses to see if Brig will initiate the next step; refer to a picture schedule before each step so Brig knows what is all done and what is coming next; and engage in the same high interest activity (e.g., watching television, snack) following the routine each day so that Brig is motivated to complete the routine.

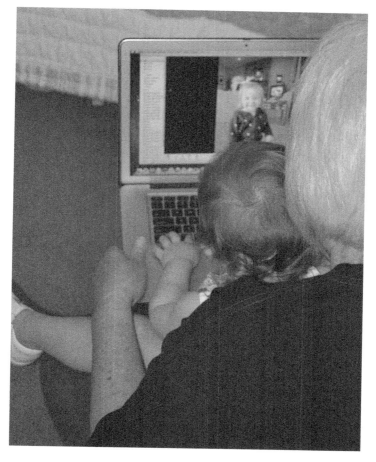

*Figure 2.1. Viewing the video*

## Child outcomes

Brig's transition up to her bedroom to complete the dressing routine drastically improved after only two weeks of watching the video (six viewing opportunities). She soon learned that, "Time to get dressed," meant that she would get to watch a video, and she started responding to that direction by walking to the bottom of the stairs. Brig was now able to remain calm throughout the entire routine. Her family was very pleased with her quick progress and they were excited to start focusing on a variety of social, self-help, and communication skills during this routine.

## Fading and generalization

Because the video was only being used three times each week, Brig continued to participate in the dressing routine four days each week without the added support that the video provided her. Once her caregivers were all comfortable with Brig's level of cooperation during this routine, they began to fade the use of the video by decreasing her viewing frequencies each week by one. The fading process took three weeks and they reported that Brig maintained her level of skills during this routine, even after the video was no longer being used. They reported that they occasionally used the video to help with the transition from playing with toys or watching a video to dressing when Brig is having an "off" day.

# JAMIRA (THREE-AND-A-HALF YEARS OLD): TOILETING

## Child background

Jamira, a three-and-a-half-year-old girl with ASD, attended a preschool classroom designed for children without disabilities three mornings per week. Within her preschool classroom, Jamira received services from a special education teacher, an autism specialist, a speech therapist, and an occupational therapist from her local school district. During the year prior to attending preschool, Jamira had received early intervention services within her home.

Jamira's family was very pleased with the progress she had made within this year. She had progressed from having a very limited vocabulary and speaking primarily in one and two-word phrases to having a large vocabulary typical of children her age. She also spoke in long, complex sentences. Despite this and other progress, Jamira's parents were frustrated with the difficulties Jamira was having with toilet training. She demonstrated all of the requisite skills for success in toilet training including knowing whether she was wet or dry, managing her clothing, using toileting words such as "poop," and "pee," and following directions. However, Jamira was unable to remain dry throughout her day. Additionally, she required heavy support to complete the toileting routine including the use of a picture sequence and physical support to sequence the steps in the routine. Jamira's parents had employed many different toilet-training strategies including using Jamira's sister as a model, having Jamira watch potty training videos, and using a reward chart. They had abandoned each of these attempts due to a lack of success and even regression. Jamira had recently begun to refuse to use the toilet at all. Using the bathroom had become a very emotionally charged routine within their household. Jamira's parents were frustrated and ready to try something different.

## Description of the video

A VSM video depicting Jamira successfully completing the toileting routine was created for a variety of reasons. Because toileting had become an emotional routine for Jamira, during which she responded negatively by protesting, yelling, or crying to any verbal prompt given to her, Jamira's educational team wanted to present a successful demonstration of Jamira independently going to the potty (free from all social interactions and prompting) to ultimately increase her skills so that less prompting would be needed for her to complete the toileting routine. The team also wanted to create the VSM video to teach Jamira the correct sequence of steps within the toileting routine; they believed that she was unclear of the accurate sequence. At this point, it was less important to Jamira's parents that Jamira actually remain dry throughout her day than for Jamira to willingly and independently try to go to the potty on a consistent schedule throughout her day.

The special education teacher at Jamira's preschool created the VSM video. Jamira's parents decided it would be better to complete the filming at school because the toileting routine had become so emotional at home. Before recording began, Jamira's parents gave written permission for her teacher to create a VSM video of Jamira completing the toileting routine. On the day of filming, Jamira's mother sent Jamira to school in a dress for increased privacy. Throughout filming, discretion was used at all times to not film below the waist unless Jamira's dress was covering her bottom. Her teacher deleted all raw footage from both the camera and the computer after the final VSM video was created. Raw footage was recorded in order to create a completed video depicting Jamira independently completing the toileting routine including the following steps: (1) entering the bathroom; (2) pulling down her underwear; (3) sitting on the toilet for 30 seconds; (4) getting an appropriate amount of toilet paper and wiping her bottom; (5) pulling up her underwear; (6) flushing the toilet; (7) washing her hands; and (8) leaving the bathroom. To create the video, the teacher held the camera while the teacher's aide helped Jamira, when needed. The teacher's aide helped Jamira begin each step. The aide helped Jamira sit on the toilet, started to pull the toilet paper and turned on the water, and then the aide stepped out of the camera focus area. During some of the taping, Jamira started crying.

At that time, her teacher framed the camera to avoid Jamira's face and instead focused on the action. Heavy editing was required because Jamira required many physical prompts to complete the routine. The verbal prompts and Jamira's crying were muted during editing and calm, instrumental music was added. At the end of the finished video, a still shot of Jamira smiling was added with a voice-over stating, "Good job, Jamira! You went to the potty all by yourself!" The edited video was two-and-a-half minutes long.

## Viewing the video

Jamira's teacher saved the completed VSM video onto the classroom's laptop computer so Jamira could watch it within the classroom. It was also burned onto a DVD so Jamira could watch it at home, either on her television or computer. Because going to the bathroom had become so challenging at home, Jamira's mother wanted Jamira to watch the video and practice going to the bathroom at school before it was introduced at home. Jamira watched the video every day at school with her special education teacher or teacher's aide just before trying to go to the potty. The bathroom was large enough, so Jamira's teacher decided to set up a viewing area consisting of two small chairs in the bathroom so Jamira would have privacy while watching her video. Jamira was instantly very interested in watching her movie. She watched the entire video without commenting on the video or looking away from the screen.

## Facilitating skill development following the video

Immediately after watching the VSM video, Jamira's teacher prompted Jamira to, "Go potty." Without delay, Jamira began pulling down her underwear to go to the potty. When Jamira tried to go to the potty after watching the video for the first time, she needed a few prompts to start the next step in the routine. For example, after getting up from the toilet, she forgot to get toilet paper and after flushing, she forgot to wash her hands. Because Jamira's parents and teachers were working toward Jamira being able to independently go to the bathroom, all prompting was done nonverbally with a point or gesture. Jamira's teacher knew that Jamira might become dependent on verbal prompts such as, "Get toilet paper." It would be easier to fade a gesture than it would be to fade a verbal prompt.

## Child outcomes

The day after the video was introduced at school, Jamira completely stopped resisting going to the potty at school. Jamira needed fewer prompts each time she tried to go potty. After two weeks of practice at school, Jamira was able to complete the entire toileting routine independently. Her mother made a point of sending Jamira to school in clothing that was easy for her to manage, such as leggings or loose pants with elastic waistbands. During this two-week time period, Jamira continued to wear training diapers to school and had voided in the toilet two times.

## Fading and generalization

After two weeks of successfully watching the video and using the bathroom at school, Jamira's mother introduced the video at home. Jamira's parents decided to have Jamira watch the video on their laptop computer at the kitchen table when she finished eating her breakfast. They did this for three reasons: (1) the kitchen was close to the bathroom so the transition to the bathroom would be quick; (2) Jamira would already be seated in her chair to better attend to her video; and (3) Jamira would be more likely to actually have to "go potty" after having eaten. Jamira's parents were anxious about how Jamira would respond to watching the video at home because toilet training had become so challenging for them. They could not have been more pleased. After watching the video for the first time at home, Jamira hopped out of her kitchen chair and padded off to the bathroom! She willingly completed the steps for going to the potty but did not actually "pee" this first time after watching the video. Jamira continued to watch her VSM video at home after breakfast every day as well as an extra time at school on school days. Four weeks after initially introducing the video at school, Jamira's teacher created a visual toileting chart indicating when Jamira should go to the potty each day (e.g., when she woke up, after breakfast, before gymnastics). Jamira continued to watch her video after breakfast but did not watch it the other times throughout the day, unless she requested it. At this time, Jamira's teachers also stopped using the video at school because Jamira began using the girls' group bathroom along with the rest of her class. Over the next month, Jamira's parents gradually stopped using the video because Jamira did not seem to need it. When they told her it was, "Time to go potty," she willingly went to the bathroom and independently completed the toileting routine. She had also begun to wear underwear throughout the day. When her parents were consistent with implementing the toileting schedule, Jamira was able to stay dry throughout the day. With the use of VSM over the span of two months, Jamira had progressed from refusing to use the toilet at all to remaining dry throughout the entire day with the use of a toileting schedule. Jamira had even begun telling her parents when she needed to "Go to potty!" Jamira's parents and teachers were ecstatic with her progress.

# ROBERT (FOUR YEARS OLD): INCREASING POSITIVE FACIAL AFFECT AND INITIATION OF PLAY
## Child background

Robert, a four-year-old boy, began receiving in-center special education services within a community preschool classroom designed for children without special needs when he was diagnosed with ASD at the age of three. Within the classroom setting, Robert received specialized support from a special education teacher, a speech and language pathologist, an autism specialist, and a teacher's aide. Robert's cognitive skills were an area of strength for him. He enjoyed talking about numbers and letters and was starting to recognize simple written words. His expressive language skills were stronger than his understanding of language. Robert used primarily three to five-word phrases to communicate his wants and needs and to make comments. He had a difficult time answering questions and responding to multi-step directions. Robert learned best when provided with visual supports. Visuals were used to teach new language concepts, to build on his current play skills, and to increase his independence with daily routines (e.g., toileting, washing hands, getting dressed). Robert had a difficult time initiating activities during free play within the classroom and needed adult support in order to make a choice and begin to play. He used a visual schedule during this time, which provided him with a plan and allowed the adults to fade their support. He seemed to enjoy being at school and participating in most activities; however, his facial affect did not always validate this. Robert's face rarely showed any emotion. There were certain physical activities that made him smile including being tickled by an adult and spinning in an adult's arms. During play in the classroom, Robert would smile and sometimes giggle if his adult play partner used exaggerated facial expressions and sounds while doing something unexpected (e.g., pretending to trip on a block and then slowly falling to the floor). Robert's flat facial affect and his difficulty initiating play really stood out in the gym. While all of the other kids were running around and having fun, Robert would stand in one spot and observe those around him. When his peers would do something silly and begin to laugh, Robert's facial expression would not change. He would follow through with an activity with adult support, but once the adult tried to fade his support, Robert would continue with that same activity for the remainder of gym time or would return to just standing around and observing others.

## Description of the video

A VSM video was created in order to increase Robert's positive facial affect and his ability to initiate play with a variety of materials while in the gym. While Robert's class played in the gym one day, his special education teacher filmed him participating in the following activities: riding a tricycle, climbing on the indoor playground equipment, rocking in a boat, running and jumping on the mats, and playing "Ring Around the Rosie." To get clips of Robert participating in these activities, his teacher would get Robert started and would continue to provide Robert with verbal support while filming. To get a clip of Robert smiling and laughing, his teacher tickled him while saying, "I'm gonna get you!" The camera only recorded his face at this time. The entire filming process took less than ten minutes because each clip was only 20–30 seconds in length. The editing process took a bit longer. The clips were spliced together to create the following sequence: (1) Robert laughing; (2) Robert riding a bike; (3) Robert laughing; (4) Robert climbing on the indoor playground equipment; (5) Robert laughing; (6) Robert rocking in a boat with three other children; (7) Robert laughing;

(8) Robert running and jumping on the mats with two other children; (9) Robert laughing; (10) Robert playing "Ring Around the Rosie" with two other children; and (11) Robert laughing. The clip of him laughing was only about five seconds and this same clip was used in all six instances. The sound on all clips was muted except for the clips of Robert laughing. An upbeat, instrumental song was added to the background of the entire video. A beginning title was added with the following text and voice-over narration, "I love the gym!" Similar voice-over narrations were also added to the clips of Robert playing (e.g., "I love to ride bikes!" "Climbing is so much fun!"). The video ended with a clip of Robert laughing and another voice-over narration that said, "I love the gym!" To make the video look more professional, a closing page was added with the following text and voice-over narration, "The end." The completed video was less than three minutes. The final video was saved on a USB flash drive.

## Viewing the video

Robert watched this video on his classroom computer each school day (his class met two days each week). He wouldn't tolerate wearing headphones, so he wasn't able to watch the video until his peers had left the classroom for the gym. This provided Robert with a distraction-free viewing environment. He didn't mind staying back in the classroom and watching his peers leave because he enjoyed watching the video so much. Robert did not require any support to remain seated and focused on the video so his special education teacher was able to work quietly in the classroom while Robert watched the video. Robert and his teacher walked to the gym as soon as the video ended.

## Facilitating skill development following the video

Robert's teacher continued to initiate his first activity in the gym each day. His teacher would use similar language to what was heard in the video to reinforce his positive affect. For example, if Robert was riding a tricycle, his teacher might have said, "You love to ride bikes!" If Robert was rocking in the boat, his teacher might have said, "Rocking in the boat is so much fun!" If Robert needed help to engage in a new activity, his teacher would provide him with two options that were shown in the video ("You can play 'Ring Around the Rosie' with Suzie or you can run and jump on the mats with George"). His teacher engaged him in tickling or swinging a few times during each 30-minute gym period because she knew this was a sure way to get him to smile and laugh.

## Child outcomes

After one month of viewing the video (eight viewing opportunities), Robert was initiating at least two activities in the gym each day. There were some days in which he would initiate up to five different activities during the 30-minute gym period. He was still observed to stand back and watch his peers; however, he was now joining in play alongside his peers when he saw something that looked like fun. He was initiating social interactions with his teachers each day in order to get more tickling or spinning. His facial affect remained quite flat when compared to his peers, but he would smile when an adult commented on his play using the phrases from the video ("It's fun to run and jump on the mats!") and sometimes when a group of children around him were acting silly and laughing.

## Fading and generalization

Following a week-long break from school in March, Robert began watching the video only one time each week. This viewing frequency continued for one month until the video was completely faded. Robert's skills continued to increase. It was soon warm outside and his class began playing outside. His facial affect and ability to initiate play had generalized to this new setting, even though he was no longer watching the video.

# AHMAD (FOUR-AND-A-HALF YEARS OLD): INITIATING PLAY WITH PEERS

## Child background

Ahmad was a four-and-a-half-year-old boy with a diagnosis of ASD. He attended a preschool classroom designed for children without disabilities four afternoons a week. Within his preschool classroom, he received services from a special education teacher, an autism specialist, and a speech therapist. Ahmad enjoyed school. He was highly verbal, participated in group-learning activities, and engaged in a variety of activities throughout the classroom. Although Ahmad responded to his peers when they initiated interactions with him, he rarely initiated conversations or play with his classmates. In addition, when he did ask a friend to play, he used a very quiet voice, making it difficult for his classmates to hear him within the noisy classroom. Ahmad's teacher decided to create a VSM video to encourage Ahmad to initiate play interactions with peers more frequently, using a louder voice.

## Description of the video

A VSM video was created depicting Ahmad asking a variety of friends to play in various areas of the classroom. To prepare for filming the video, Ahmad's teacher had Ahmad practice asking his teachers to play. A picture of a person using a loud voice was shown to Ahmad to remind him to use a "big voice" when speaking. After role-playing with his teacher a few times, filming began. His teacher had decided that she would film Ahmad and the teacher's aide would provide verbal prompts, as needed, while Ahmad asked friends to play. When filming began, the teacher's aide directed Ahmad to ask his friend, Josie, to paint at the easel. The aide told Ahmad the exact words to use, showed him the "big voice" visual, and then stepped out of the camera focus area. Ahmad asked Josie, "Do you want to paint at the easel?" When Josie said, "Yes," the teacher's aide told the two children to walk to the easel together and begin painting. The teacher filmed the children walking to the easel together and briefly filmed Ahmad and Josie painting at the easel together. When Ahmad was done painting, his aide directed him to ask another friend to play with him. Ahmad decided to ask his friend, Will, to play in the kitchen area. As before, the teacher's aide told Ahmad the exact words to use, showed him his "big voice" visual, and then stepped out of the camera focus area. After filming the prompted interaction as before, Ahmad was directed to ask his friend, Peter, to play with cars. All three scenarios were later edited together to depict Ahmad independently asking three different friends to play, walking to that area of the room, and beginning to play. The verbal prompts directing the kids to walk to the correct play area were muted. Any images of the teacher's aide were deleted from the final video. No voice-over narration was added except at the beginning that labeled the video as, "Ahmad asks his friends to play!" At the end of the video, Ahmad's teacher recorded her voice stating, "Good job using a big voice to ask friends to play, Ahmad!" The final video was two minutes long.

## Viewing the video

Ahmad's VSM play video was saved onto Ahmad's teacher's iPad. Ahmad watched the video every day at school at the beginning of play time. He sat with his teacher in a quiet area of the classroom. Ahmad quietly watched the video and was then directed to go ask a friend to play.

## Facilitating skill development following the video

The first time Ahmad watched his VSM video, he needed help choosing a friend to ask to play with him. His teacher asked him who he wanted to play with, what he wanted to do with them, and reminded him to just walk over and use a "big voice." He did a great job! He even took the friend's hand to walk to the play area. After playing with the friend for a while, Ahmad moved to another area of the room. His teacher then asked him if he would like to play with a different friend. Ahmad said, "I want to play with Will." He independently walked over to Will and asked him to play with the blocks!

## Child outcomes

Ahmad's VSM video worked beautifully. He continued to watch the video every day at the beginning of play time and needed fewer and fewer prompts each day to ask a friend to play. He consistently used a "big voice" when speaking with his classmates. The visual that his teacher had made to remind him to use a loud-enough voice was no longer necessary.

## Fading and generalization

After watching the video every school day for two weeks, the video was faded from use. Ahmad was independently approaching his peers and consistently speaking loudly enough to be heard. One unexpected benefit was that Ahmad had begun to initiate play interactions with his classmates while in the gym and in the playground. He had also begun to speak louder throughout his school day such as during circle time and snack time. Ahmad also began to generalize these skills to home. His mother said he had asked his cousin to play with him while he was at his house. His mother was delighted to see Ahmad initiate play!

# JEAN (SIX YEARS OLD): REDUCING ANXIETY

## Child background

Jean, a six-year-old girl with ASD, suffered from tremendous anxiety. The objects, activities, and environments that caused her the greatest anxiety varied greatly over time. While some of her fears were things that commonly caused anxiety in young children such as visits to the doctor and separating from parents, many of her fears were related to harmless things including being near other children and balloons. Her reactions to the things that made her nervous were often exaggerated in length and degree. Her parents, as well as her educational team (e.g., special education teacher, autism specialist, private therapy providers), tried all possible strategies that were appropriate for her level of functioning. Jean's cognitive and motor skills were an area of strength for her. Her language and social interaction skills were her two areas of greatest need. She was able to effectively communicate her wants and needs to others and was able to engage in basic conversations. She enjoyed interacting with familiar adults and peers, but needed adult support in order to appropriately initiate and maintain interactions. The use of picture schedules and social narratives were helpful to decrease her anxiety to some extent, but there were still some activities that her parents avoided because of how stressful it was for the entire family. One activity that her family enjoyed doing together was playing in the neighborhood park. However, Jean developed a fear of this park and playing there was no longer an enjoyable experience. Jean would engage in repeated questioning about whether or not the park was on her schedule for the day and would become agitated if her parents even drove anywhere near it. At the park, Jean's heart would race and she would cry uncontrollably. Jean's parents' main priority during the last few weeks of school was to decrease Jean's anxiety related to playing in their neighborhood park.

## Description of the video

A VSM video was created to increase Jean's ability to play in her neighborhood park while remaining calm. In order to make this video, clips of Jean playing at the park needed to be recorded. One morning, Jean's mother put a picture of a park on Jean's daily schedule and let Jean know exactly when they would be going to the park that day. She also put together a picture schedule that described exactly what they would do at the park. The activities pictured on the schedule included looking at the ducks, swinging on the swings, digging in the sand, going down the slide, running down the hill, and running around the bases on the baseball field. These were all activities that Jean had enjoyed at the park just weeks earlier. When Jean started asking questions about the park and requesting that they not go, her mother reviewed the daily schedule with Jean as well as the list of what they would do at the park. Her mother did not engage in any conversations with her regarding the park. Instead, she told Jean that it was alright to be nervous and modeled some calm-down strategies including squeezing her hands, rubbing her legs, and taking deep breaths. She also gave Jean some calming phrases to use such as, "It's no big deal," so Jean would have a way to consistently respond to her own anxious feelings. Both the daily schedule and the picture schedule describing the activities planned for the park were brought to the park with them. Jean began crying as soon as her mother pulled into the park's parking lot. Jean cried on and off during their visit to the park but seemed to benefit from her picture schedules. Her mother recorded short video clips of Jean participating in each activity. When possible, Jean was recorded from behind so that her sad face was not shown. The filming took less than 15 minutes. The video clips were saved on a USB flash drive and were given to Jean's special education teacher for editing.

During the editing process, a title page was added to the beginning of the video with the following text and voice-over narration, "I love the park." The middle of the video consisted of clips of Jean playing at the park. All video clips were muted and one of Jean's favorite songs was added to the background of the entire video. At the end of all video clips, a still frame of Jean smiling was added with the following voice-over narration, "Good job, Jean! You had so much fun at the park!" An audio clip of kids cheering was also added while this picture was still on the screen. Closing text was added to the end of the video with the following voice-over narration, "The end." The finished video was just over three minutes and was burned to a DVD.

## Viewing the video

Jean's nanny showed her this video three times each week. She watched it on a television while sitting on a couch in her family room. She was very interested in watching the video and sometimes asked to watch it again. Her nanny typically allowed this. The video was shown at different times each day depending on their daily schedule. They went to the park to play at least two times each week immediately following the viewing.

### Facilitating skill development following the video

Jean's nanny used the same strategies mentioned earlier (i.e., picture schedule, consistent calm-down strategy, and calming phrases) when Jean would become upset over having to go to the park. Jean was allowed to choose the order of activities at the park and she typically wanted to do things in the same order each day. Her nanny viewed this as a coping strategy and decided to address her rigidity at a later time.

### Child outcomes

After only four viewings and two trips to the park, Jean was able to tolerate seeing the park on her daily schedule and played at the park while remaining calm. When someone would mention going to the park, instead of pleading to not go, Jean would say, "I love the park!" The progress she made in less than two weeks was remarkable. Her parents were thrilled with the results of VSM and were excited to make additional videos to address her other fears.

### Fading and generalization

Jean continued to watch the video two or three times each week throughout the months of June and July and visited the park at least one time each week. Toward the end of the summer, Jean no longer watched the video on a consistent basis and her anxiety related to playing in her neighborhood park began to increase.

We believe that videos created to reduce anxiety may need to be shown for longer periods of time and gradually and systematically faded in order to maintain the reduced levels of anxiety.

# 3

# POINT-OF-VIEW VIDEO MODELING (PVM)

Point-of-view Video Modeling (PVM) is similar to Basic Video Modeling (BVM) in that it involves recording a person other than the learner, such as a parent, sibling, teacher, or peer, engaging in the specific skill or routine that you are targeting. The one thing that sets this strategy apart from the other forms of video modeling (and ultimately gives it its name) is the fact that the recording captures exactly what the learner will see through his own eyes while demonstrating the skill or routine. Given that the recording illustrates the targeted skill from the learner's point of view, the video typically only includes the model's hands (e.g., demonstrating how to play with a specific toy) as well as any social partners that are necessary for the skill or routine to be demonstrated. One example of an instance in which you would need to include a social partner in the video is when modeling how to appropriately respond to a greeting. In this situation, you might film a peer walking up to the camera saying, "Hi," followed by the person filming the video waving and saying, "Hi," in return. These videos are then viewed by the learner to provide a powerful visual model of exactly what is expected of him while demonstrating a skill or routine.

PVM videos are an effective way to teach any new skill that the learner is not yet able to demonstrate without a substantial amount of adult support because the learner is not the one performing the skill in the video. These videos are also a good way to teach social interaction skills that require eye gaze in a certain direction.

An example of a skill that requires the learner's eye gaze to be in a certain direction is responding to his name. In this situation, the person filming could start recording with the camera pointing toward a set of toys. The only thing being captured is the hand of the person filming while playing with the toys. An actor is needed to call the child's name from a few feet away. Once the name is called, the person filming should stop playing with the toys and shift the camera in order to capture the person who called the child's name.

There are many advantages of PVM, both for the person filming and for the learner. For the person filming, it is almost always possible to record this type of video from start to finish in one errorless take, which means no editing! This substantially reduces the amount of time and effort that goes into making the video and allows you to start using the strategy immediately. For the learner, PVM allows him to watch and learn without needing to understand that people have different perspectives, which can be challenging for children with autism spectrum disorders (ASD). Anytime a child watches a video that contains an actor, there is a chance he will need to understand the actor's perspective (or point of view) in order to fully benefit from the video. This is never an issue when using PVM. Because this type of video captures only what the learner will actually see through his own eyes, it is easy to control the number of distractions within the video. This allows the learner to watch the video without having to discern what information is important and what is not, which can also be challenging for learners with ASD.

## STEPS TO POINT-OF-VIEW VIDEO MODELING

We have identified ten steps that are important to follow when using PVM with young children. These steps are described in detail below. While some of the steps may be the same or similar to those involved in BVM and Video Self-Modeling (VSM), there are many components that are specific to creating PVM videos.

# Step One: Identify a skill or routine that you would like to target

The first step in PVM is identifying the skill or routine that you would like to target. Remember, the expected behaviors that make up the skill or routine must be within the child's reach. While this list is not exhaustive, we hope it gives you some ideas of where to start if you don't already have a skill in mind.

- Functional play with toys

- Creative play with toys

- Taking turns during play with a toy or game

- Tracing lines, shapes, letters, etc.

- Writing a name

- Drawing a simple picture

- Appropriate tool use (e.g., spoon, fork, markers, scissors)

- Washing hands

- Putting on socks, shoes, pants

- Lining up at the door behind peers

- Walking in line with peers

- Stopping at the door and waiting for a teacher

- Tidying toys, after a snack, etc.

- Shifting attention to imitate a play partner's actions

- Referencing a social partner and following their nonverbal cues (e.g., eye gaze, point)

- Responding to name when called

- Responding to greetings

## Step Two: Identify and assemble
## the materials needed

There are many things to consider when identifying and assembling the materials needed. If you are going to be the actor in the video and the skill or routine you are targeting requires the use of two hands, you may need another person to operate the camera. If you can't find someone to help, you might be able to capture the child's point of view by placing the camera on a tripod. This is only an option when targeting a skill in which the child's eye gaze will remain in one spot, such as functional play with a toy or cutting with scissors. If you happen to have a camera that attaches to a head-strap mount, this would be the perfect time to use it! Remember to gather all materials that are necessary for the skill or routine to be completed (e.g., toys, scissors, socks, shoes).

At this time, you should also think about how you will show the video to the child. Video playback options include a television, computer, portable DVD player, electronic tablet, smartphone, video-recording device, etc. The way in which you choose to show the video to the child will determine what equipment is needed when saving the video (DVD, USB flash drive, etc.).

## Step Three: Complete a task analysis of the skill or
## routine and collect baseline data

Task analysis is just a fancy phrase that represents the process of breaking down a skill or routine in order to identify its smallest elements (each expected behavior). For example, the smallest elements involved in hand washing may include approaching the sink, stepping up onto a stool, turning on the water, getting soap, scrubbing hands, rinsing off the soap, turning off the water, stepping down from the stool, getting a paper towel, drying hands, and putting the paper towel in the garbage. It is important to determine if there are any elements of the target skill that the child can already independently demonstrate. Sit back and observe the child demonstrating the skill prior to intervention. This is considered collecting baseline data. If you find that the child can complete some of the steps at the beginning of the routine independently (e.g., approaching the sink and stepping up onto the stool), it may not be necessary to include these steps in the video.

## Step Four: Make a plan for the filming of the video

The first step to making a plan for filming is determining which type of video to make. See Appendix A for more information regarding how to best match the type of video modeling to the child as well as to the skill or routine that you are targeting. Once this is determined, make an outline for the video that includes everything that you will do from start to finish. See Appendix B for several sample outlines. If you are in charge of filming and another person is the actor, you will need to make sure that the actor understands exactly what you want her to do. In regards to the language used in the video, don't forget to discuss the amount (e.g., no talking, some talking, lots of talking) and level (e.g., one-word phrases, two-word phrases, three to four-word phrases) you want included in the video prior to filming. In most of our PVM videos, our actors use words while demonstrating the skill to highlight the important elements. For example, if you are making a video to target hand washing, you may want the actor to say things such as, "Turn water on," and "Rub hands together." We also suggest using language that is at or slightly above the expressive language abilities of the child. If the child speaks in primarily one-word phrases, try to limit your language to one, two and three-word phrases.

## Step Five: Record the video

Recording a PVM video will look different depending upon who is doing the filming. If someone is available to help you during this step, ask him to hold the camera next to the side of your head so that it captures the skill or routine from the child's point of view. If you choose to use a tripod, make sure that the camera is positioned slightly behind your body but close to the height of your head. The length of each video will depend upon the skill being modeled as well as the attention abilities of the child. We recommend, however, that each video be no longer than three minutes.

## Step Six: Edit the video footage

As mentioned earlier, one of the big advantages of PVM is that editing most likely is not required. Typically, it is possible to record a PVM video from start to finish in one continuous and errorless take. If you feel as though editing is required, please refer to the editing process described in Chapter 1.

## Step Seven: Show the video to the child

Whether you are showing the video in the child's home, out in the community, or in a classroom, there are many options for video playback. As mentioned earlier, these options include your television, computer, portable DVD player, electronic tablet, smartphone, video-recording device, etc. As explained in earlier chapters, it is important to give the child the opportunity to watch the video in its entirety without interruption. This may be easier to accomplish in the child's home. If the child is watching the video at school, it might be best to play it on a portable device in a quiet area of the classroom (or in the hall if one cannot be found) or on the classroom computer using headphones.

Every child is different and may benefit from different frequencies of viewing. Some may need to watch the video every day, while others may demonstrate progress when only given a few opportunities to watch the video each week. If possible, allow the child to watch the video immediately prior to practicing the skill. If the video targets walking down the hall at school, the child should watch the video right before his class lines up to walk down the hall. If this adds one extra transition that is difficult for the child, the video can be shown at a different time (e.g., at home before going to school or after he is done playing on the computer, but before he moves onto the next play station).

## Step Eight: Facilitate skill development following the viewing of the video

It is important for you to continue facilitating the child's skill development following the viewing of the video. For example, if you are targeting the child's ability to independently wash his hands, don't just show him the video and then send him into the bathroom to wash his hands on his own. Continue to support his skills by providing him with visual supports (e.g., a picture sequence illustrating the steps to be completed), nonverbal prompts (e.g., point toward the faucet to remind him what he needs to do next), and praise. PVM should not replace, but rather add to, the strategies that you are currently using to target an increase in the child's skills. While the effects of PVM are often remarkable, it is not a quick fix and will not always immediately increase the child's skills.

## Step Nine: Monitor the child's progress to determine if changes need to be made

We highly recommend that you monitor the child's progress after you begin showing him the video. Record data on the child's ability to demonstrate all of the expected behaviors that make up the skill or routine that you are targeting. This will give you concrete evidence to look back upon when determining whether the child is making progress as quickly as you had hoped. See Appendix C for sample data sheets that may be useful to you in monitoring progress.

## Step Ten: Problem solve if progress is slow

If the child's progress is slow, we recommend engaging in some problem solving before changing your video or discontinuing its use. There are many things to consider when the child's skills are not progressing as you would have hoped. You may find it helpful to ask yourself some of the following questions.

- Are you showing the video as often as needed?

- Is there a better time within the child's day that the video could be shown?

- Is the environment in which the child is watching the video too distracting?

- Is the video too long?

- Would a different type of video modeling work better to increase the child's ability to demonstrate the target skill?

- Does the skill that you are targeting include too many steps or expected behaviors that are too far out of the child's reach?

If you choose to make changes, you should begin by adjusting only one variable (e.g., the frequency in which the video is shown) and then continue to monitor the child's progress. If the child's progress increases then you may have solved the problem! If the child's progress continues to be slow, try adjusting another variable (e.g., the time of day the child watches the video). If you make too many changes at once it will be difficult to determine what change made the biggest impact. If you can target the change that made the biggest impact, it will increase the effectiveness of all subsequent videos.

## POINT-OF-VIEW VIDEO MODELING CASE STUDIES

Now that you know the steps involved in PVM, it's time to share with you some real-life examples that describe how we have used PVM to target a change in the behaviors of young children with ASD. The following six case studies are arranged in ascending order by the age of the child, from 23 months up to 5 years.

### RITA (23 MONTHS OLD): EXPRESSIVE LANGUAGE
#### Child background

Rita began receiving in-home early intervention services after she was diagnosed with ASD at the age of 23 months. At that time, her parents identified her expressive language skills as their main concern. They felt as though Rita was growing more frustrated each day due to her very limited ability to communicate her wants and needs to others. Rita's favorite things to play with were balls and she was able to request them by saying, "Ba." Rita's parents were able to list 19 other words that they had heard her say; however, these words were rarely used to make requests or to label the things Rita saw. Instead, the words were used nonfunctionally throughout her day. Rita was often heard to repeat a word multiple times when that object was nowhere in sight and while she was happily engaged in a daily routine. For example, her parents shared that she would sometimes say, "Car," five to ten times while eating lunch, but there was no car in sight and she seemed content with what she was currently doing. There were times when it seemed as though Rita was using a word to make a request; however, she was not yet able to coordinate her words with an eye gaze toward her listener. Rita's ability to follow basic one-step directions was inconsistent. It was best when paired with a visual cue such as pointing into the bucket while saying, "Put in." Rita's parents kept her schedule fairly consistent each day. This contributed to her ability to transition between activities as well as her ability to cooperate and participate in most daily routines.

## Description of the video

A PVM video was created to increase Rita's ability to use her words to request items during daily snacks and meals. Prior to filming, her mother created a list of ten food items to be included in the video. She chose the items based on Rita's food preferences as well as the difficulty level of the word. The chosen food items included chicken, fries, toast, cracker, cheerios, cookie, chips, apple, milk, and juice. The video was filmed in Rita's kitchen during a regularly scheduled home visit. While sitting on a chair next to the kitchen table, the person filming pressed record when the camera was looking down toward an empty plate. The camera then shifted up to Rita's mother who was standing beside the table and focused on her face while the person filming said, "Chicken." Rita's mother responded by saying, "Sure. Here's chicken." She reached over the table and placed the chicken on the empty plate as the camera shifted down to focus on her hand placing the chicken on the plate. The person filming picked up the chicken and brought it up to her mouth while making eating sounds. She modeled the word one or two more times while pretending to eat the chicken through phrases such as, "Mmm, chicken," or "Yummy chicken!" The camera remained focused on the empty plate at this time and only showed the hand picking up the chicken. This sequence was repeated with each of the food items. The verbal requests made by the person filming were somewhat varied and included primarily one and two-word phrases such as, "Mom, fries," "More toast," "Cracker," and "Cheerios, please." Rita's mother varied her responses as well. This video was two minutes and fifty seconds in length and required no editing.

### Viewing the video

The video was saved onto the family's computer at the end of the home visit. It was decided that Rita would watch the video prior to eating breakfast each day. It was explained that Rita's full attention should be on the video and that she should be allowed to watch it from beginning to end without interruption. The next day, Rita's mother reported that she placed Rita in her booster seat at the kitchen table and set their laptop on the table. Rita seemed interested in the video and her mother refrained from verbally responding to her smiles and gestures toward the computer screen to keep her focused on the video. Rita's mother did respond nonverbally by smiling and then pointing and looking toward the screen.

### Facilitating skill development following the video

Following each viewing, Rita's mother followed through with their meal time routine. Rita was given an empty plate and her mother sat next to her with a few food items for Rita to choose. If Rita didn't automatically reach out for one of the foods, her mother would hold up two items while offering her a choice (e.g., "Cheerios or toast?"). If Rita made a choice by reaching for one item, her mother would hold up that food item, point to it, model the word ("Toast!") and pause for two to three seconds to allow Rita to imitate the word. If Rita said the word, she was reinforced by her mother placing the food on her plate. If she didn't say the word, Rita's mother would model the word two or three more times while moving the food closer to her, eventually placing it on Rita's plate. Rita's mother was instructed to pause between each model of the word in order to give Rita time to respond. If Rita did not make a choice by reaching for an item, her mother would make the choice and hold the item up while following through with the same sequence of modeling the word, then pausing. Instead of giving Rita an entire piece of toast or a bowl full of Cheerios, her mother would give her small amounts in order to increase the number of times a request could be practiced. While Rita was eating the food, her mother would model the phrases from the video such as "Mmm, toast," or "Yummy toast!"

## Child outcomes

Rita's mother reported that Rita began to use some words modeled in the video after only 11 days of watching it. She would say the words in nonfunctional ways during other daily routines and she would also imitate some of the words during meals. After two to three weeks of watching the video, Rita was spontaneously using one-word phrases to request a few different food items during meals. She inconsistently coordinated her words with an eye gaze toward her mother. Rita's parents were very pleased with her progress and continued to show her the video on most days.

## Fading and generalization

Rita stopped watching this video after two months mainly because her parents had new priorities, which initiated the creation of new videos for her to watch. Rita continued to increase her language during meals, plus her ability to coordinate her eye gaze with her words was improving. With continued services from an early childhood special education team that targeted an increase in her use of language, Rita's expressive vocabulary increased to more than 50 words in only a few months. Her mother felt that the snack and meal time video had supported Rita's increase in spontaneous language during other daily routines. She also reported that the video was a good reminder to her and to Rita's other caregivers to keep their language simple while interacting with Rita. Rita was observed in her preschool setting three months following the introduction of the video. At that time, she was spontaneously making requests for more snack items using one-word phrases. Her eye contact while requesting was inconsistent. Her eye contact was best when her teacher provided wait time before giving Rita what she requested.

## JOHN (TWO-AND-A-HALF YEARS OLD): FUNCTIONAL PLAY AND INCREASED ATTENTION
### Child background

John, a two-and-a-half-year-old boy, began receiving in-home special education services at the age of 21 months under the educational category of ASD. At that point, John had an expressive vocabulary of approximately 60 words and spoke primarily in one-word phrases. He understood some basic one-step directions that were given on a daily basis (e.g., get your shoes, get the wipes, time to eat), but followed through with them inconsistently. He demonstrated frequent tantrums when he didn't get what he wanted, could be aggressive (e.g., biting, hitting, throwing toys) with both children and adults, and needed constant adult supervision in order to keep his body safe. Transitions between daily activities often brought out many of the previously mentioned unexpected behaviors such as biting and hitting. His ability to transition was best when his family followed a consistent schedule each day. John needed a lot of support in order to regulate his sensory system each day. He was impulsive and his ability to remain engaged in age-appropriate activities was very limited. He enjoyed playing with toys, but needed heavy adult support in order to maintain his attention for longer than a few minutes. When playing with an adult, John would appropriately shift his attention away from the materials in order to observe the adult's actions. He would imitate simple play actions that were repeated often and that were accompanied by silly noises and/or exaggerated expressions. Without adult support, John had the tendency to dump out the play materials, hoard them close to his body, repeat one or two basic play actions over and over again, and/or throw the materials.

## Description of the video

A PVM video was created for John to increase his ability to play functionally with one set of toys over an extended period of time. The video was approximately two minutes in length and included three toy cars and five primary-colored cardboard blocks. In the video, the following three basic play strategies were modeled on a table: (1) placing the blocks in a row to create a road and pushing the cars on the road; (2) building a tunnel and pushing the cars through the tunnel; and (3) building a garage and parking the cars inside. During the video, the actor used simple language consisting of primarily two and three-word phrases. The video began with the actor saying, "Time to play with cars," and then taking the materials out of a plastic tub. The video ended with the actor saying, "All done cars," and then placing the materials back into the plastic tub while singing a clean-up song. John's early intervention teacher created the video. Because there was no one available to assist her at the time of filming, she placed the camera on a tripod that stood slightly behind her and to her right. The camera was at the level of her head and was tilted down to include only her hands and the play materials. No editing was needed in order for this video to be effective.

## Viewing the video

The video was burned to a DVD and given to John's family along with the same set of blocks used in the video. The family had their own toy cars as well as a container to keep them in, so some of the materials were slightly different than what was shown in the video. John was shown the video on his family's home computer while sitting in his highchair. The highchair was used so that John didn't have access to any of the buttons on the computer and also to support him in remaining seated and focused on the video. John was very interested in the video and frequently shifted his attention away from the computer screen to check in with his mother and teacher. In order for him to watch the video from start to finish without distractions, his mother and teacher maintained their visual attention on the video and didn't respond to his initiations of joint attention toward the video. It was decided that John would watch the video one time each day in order to maintain consistency in his schedule across each day. Each viewing would be followed by an opportunity to play with the cars and blocks.

## Facilitating skill development following the video

Immediately following the viewing of the video, John was prompted to go into the playroom to play with the blocks and cars. In order to set him up for success, his mother organized the playroom so there would be fewer items to distract him. She put each set of materials in a separate bin and then placed the bins on a toy shelf. The large toys that didn't fit into the bins (e.g., car ramp) were placed in the closet. His mother initiated the activity with the same phrase used in the video ("Time to play with cars") and then placed the container of blocks and cars on a small train table. John's mother was instructed to begin modeling the play strategies that were shown in the video. At first, John was interested but soon resorted to gathering the cars and engaging in filling and dumping. Without knowing how it would affect John's ability to play with these materials, his mother had placed all of his toy cars in the container with the blocks. Less is often more when working with young children with John's developmental profile. Therefore, his mother was given the suggestion of limiting the number of cars in the container to five. John's mother reported that this had a tremendous impact on his ability to engage in appropriate play with the materials following the showing of the video. Another important factor that positively influenced his skills and set him up for greater success was the use of the train table. The table provided him with a visual of where he was to play with the toys and helped to better organize his body during play.

## Child outcomes

When asked about John's play skills during his next scheduled home visit (seven days following his first viewing), John's mother reported a variety of positive changes. She shared that she was now able to sit back and follow John's lead during play because he was spontaneously initiating the functional play strategies that were modeled in the video. This increase in varied play strategies had a positive effect on his ability to maintain his attention toward this set of materials. She did report that he would continue to wander away from the table after a few minutes of playing with the materials. However, it was easy to re-engage him in play by modeling the strategies shown in the video. John's mother was pleased to be spending less time struggling to engage him in appropriate play and more time sitting back and observing as well as modeling new play strategies that were not shown in the video. She also shared that she had noticed an increase in John's expressive language skills. After one short week of viewing the video, John started to spontaneously and functionally use some of the two-word phrases heard in the video while playing with the materials. This was an added benefit as the video was not made to target an increase in expressive language. It was also determined that the video most likely played a role in his stress-free transition into the playroom to play with the materials.

## Fading and generalization

John continued to enjoy watching the video each day. His mother continued to observe an increase in skills, therefore the video was never systematically faded. However, his mother was no longer adamant about showing him the video each day. She reported that, over time, John continued to demonstrate higher level skills during play with the cars and blocks with or without the use of the video. John attended a preschool program two mornings each week and was observed to have generalized his functional play with cars and blocks into this setting.

# BILLIE (THREE YEARS OLD):
# INDEPENDENT, STRUCTURED PLAY
## Child background

Billie, a three-year-old girl recently diagnosed with ASD, had been receiving early intervention services in her home under the category of developmental delay for almost one year. She was a very active little girl who had an extremely hard time sitting still or engaging in functional play. She exhibited many sensory-seeking behaviors including climbing, dropping to the floor, and banging her head. She had such a high level of activity that her parents had to completely "Billie-proof" their home for her safety. They did not have dining room chairs because Billie quickly learned to climb up onto the table. Billie's bedroom was a bare room with only a mattress on the floor. She didn't have many toys available to her because her independent play skills consisted of mouthing, throwing, and dumping. Given appropriate seating, a decreased number of toys present, and verbal and physical prompts, Billie was able to put rings on a stacker, insert coins in a slot, stack interconnecting blocks, and place pegs in a pegboard. Even with support, Billie had limited ability to maintain attention long enough to complete more than two or three repetitions. Her language skills included using familiar two-word phrases and following routine one-step directions such as, "Sit down," and "Put in." Billie's parents shared their wish for Billie to be able to play more appropriately with toys and to be able to play alone for a few minutes. The educational team decided to introduce Play Boxes to increase Billie's independent, functional skills at home. Billie would also be given the opportunity to generalize this skill into her preschool classroom.

"Play Boxes," sometimes called work or task boxes, is part of a structured teaching strategy familiar to many families and professionals who work with children on the autism spectrum. Play Boxes are simply a sequence of bins, drawers, or boxes. They are used to teach children to sequence a series of tasks. The boxes give visual structure and clarity to children in order to increase their independence and task completion skills. The boxes are put side by side with one play item in each box. The items need to have a clear beginning and ending and the child must already demonstrate the skills needed to complete the tasks. Example play items include pegs, puzzles, ring stackers, interlocking bricks, and shape sorters. Please see Figure 3.1 for an example of Play Boxes.

*Figure 3.1. An example of Play Boxes*

## Description of the video

It was decided that PVM would likely be an effective and efficient strategy to teach Billie to use Play Boxes, first because she loved to watch videos, and second because the resulting video would be free of distractions. There would not be the face of an actor on-screen to distract Billie, just the hands completing the tasks.

To get started, the family gathered tubs and toys from their home. The family chose a low table in the living room as the location where Billie would complete her Play Boxes. The toys chosen for the video were three of Billie's favorites and ones that she already knew how to play with: a ring stacker, pegs, and a shape sorter. The boxes were set up side by side with the materials taken apart. A two-minute video was recorded demonstrating the play box routine from Billie's perspective. The video camera was held by Billie's mother next to the teacher's head and was focused on the teacher's hands. The video showed the teacher's hands as she took the first tub, completed the task of putting all the rings on the ring stacker, then put the tub back. She then took the next tub, completed the task of putting all the pegs in the pegboard, then put it back and so on. During the video, the teacher made simple comments to explain what she was doing: "Time for Play Boxes," "Get box," "Put rings on," "Put box back," "Get next box," etc. This video required no editing as it was recorded in one continuous, errorless take.

### Viewing the video

The completed video was given to Billie's family on a DVD during her next home visit. A DVD, instead of a USB flash drive, allowed the family to choose to watch the video on either a television or on a computer. Her parents were told that Billie should watch the video without comment or distraction in the living room right before she completed her boxes. If Billie needed help with an item or needed to be redirected back to the boxes, her parents should do so nonverbally by pointing or by using a hand-over-hand method; it was important that Billie not become dependent on verbal prompts in order to complete the boxes.

### Child outcomes

Billie's mother was excited to introduce the video and Play Boxes to Billie. She reported that Billie loved the video! The first time Billie attempted her boxes after watching the video, she needed moderate help to complete the play sequence. Billie became frustrated with one of the items and reverted to throwing the toys to the floor. Her mother then facilitated Billie's play with hand-over-hand assistance during that one activity. Billie's mother thought the video and the Play Boxes were a huge success. It was the first time that Billie had functionally played with toys without needing a lot of support. Billie quickly learned to sequence the three tasks.

## Fading and generalization

Billie continued to watch her video at home each day and increased her independence in completing the play box sequence. She began attending her preschool class one month after the PVM video was first introduced at home. She generalized her new skills to school even though the video and materials used at school were different than at home. At school, Billie watched a similar Play Box video each day before completing the classroom Play Boxes. When the teacher changed the toys in the classroom Play Boxes every week, it was not necessary to create a new video for each set of toys. Because the items placed in the boxes were simple activities that Billie already knew how to complete, Billie was able to use the video as a visual reminder of how to complete the independent routine of the Play Boxes. After one month of watching her PVM video three times a week at school and once a week at home, Billie was able to complete the Play Boxes requiring no more than two verbal prompts throughout the routine. The educational team continues to use video modeling to teach Billie a variety of new skills, both at home and at school.

# AYLA (THREE-AND-A-HALF YEARS OLD): ART PROJECT
## Child background

Ayla began receiving in-home early intervention services through her school district when she was two years old after receiving a medical diagnosis of ASD. At three-and-a-half years of age, Ayla began attending a preschool class for children with special needs within her school district. At preschool, Ayla received services from a special education teacher, a speech therapist, an occupational therapist, and an autism specialist. Upon entering school, Ayla had an expressive vocabulary of about 70 words. She used routine two-word phrases such as, "More cracker," and "Wash hands," although she primarily communicated in one-word utterances. Ayla followed familiar one-step directions such as, "Sit down," and "Socks on." Ayla demonstrated very limited functional use of classroom art tools. She was able to make marks on paper with a marker or crayon, but did not use dot markers, paint rollers, or a paintbrush. When given these tools, Ayla quickly threw them to the floor. It was difficult to teach her to use these tools because Ayla did not tolerate hand-over-hand support and was not yet observing adults or peers using tools in order to learn new skills through imitation.

## Description of the video

A PVM video was created to help Ayla learn to make vertical strokes with a paintbrush at the easel. The easel was set up with paper taped securely to it. Two spill-proof paint containers, each a different color, and one paintbrush were placed in the easel tray. To film the video, Ayla's special education teacher held the camera next to her own face to film her free hand using the paintbrush and completing all of the actions from what would be Ayla's point of view. In the video, the actions of picking up the brush, dipping it in the paint container, and painting vertical lines were filmed. The same actions were then recorded with the second color. At the beginning of the video, the actor stated, "Time to paint," and at the end of the video the actor stated, "All done painting." Throughout the video, the actor labeled the actions including, "Get brush," "Dip, dip, dip," and "Paint up and down." When using the second color, the actor said, "All done red. Get blue paint. Dip, dip, dip." The video was one-and-a-half minutes long and was filmed in one continuous session that did not require editing.

## Viewing the video

The video was saved onto a laptop computer that was used in Ayla's preschool classroom for video modeling. It was also saved on a USB flash drive so it could be shared with Ayla's family at home. Ayla's family planned to watch the video on the family's computer so saving it to a USB flash drive was sufficient. If they had intended to watch the video on their home television, the video could have been saved to a DVD. In the classroom, the easel was set up near a small table on which the laptop computer was placed. Ayla sat with an adult and watched the video before she painted at the easel. Ayla was interested in the video but repeatedly tried to grab the materials at the easel. For future viewings, the easel was placed out of Ayla's reach. After watching the video, the adult told Ayla, "Time to paint," and directed Ayla toward the easel.

## Facilitating skill development following the video

After watching the video for the first time, Ayla picked up the brush and dipped it repeatedly into the paint container. She then banged the brush roughly on the paper several times before dropping it onto the floor. It was a start, although Ayla's painting technique needed to be refined. Even with adult support to keep her standing in front of the easel, it seemed challenging for Ayla to coordinate her body placement while using the tools appropriately. Therefore, it was decided that Ayla should sit on a chair in front of the easel. Following successive opportunities to watch the PVM video and paint at the easel while sitting, Ayla continued to dip the brush and bang it against the easel. She was having difficulty learning the technique of brushing up and down and would not tolerate the adult using hand-over-hand assistance. To address this issue, another brush was added to the easel and the adult modeled painting up and down with the second brush.

## Child outcomes

After watching the PVM video and practicing the skills for two weeks at school and after watching the video twice at home, Ayla was able to dip the brush to get paint and make several brush strokes on the paper at the easel. This was a huge improvement in Ayla's skills; prior to watching the video she simply threw the brush. Another added benefit was the increase in Ayla's imitation skills as she had learned through imitation to make both horizontal and circular strokes. The video was not intended to target imitation skills, rather to only teach Ayla to make vertical strokes at the easel. Ayla continued to drop the brush onto the floor when she was all done painting; putting the brush back into the container remained inconsistent. When the adult felt that Ayla was close to being all done painting, it was helpful to sing the clean-up song as a cue for Ayla to put the brush back into the easel tray. The skill of appropriately bringing closure to an activity continued to be challenging for Ayla throughout her day. Ayla's teachers and parents addressed this behavior by creating a different modeling video targeting that particular skill and by teaching Ayla to sign and say, "All done," instead of throwing the items she was using.

### Fading and generalization

Ayla generalized the skill of using a paintbrush at the easel to painting at the table. After six weeks, the use of the video was successfully faded within the classroom. Ayla's mother continues to use the PVM video at home prior to painting; she has found that it helps prepare Ayla for the upcoming activity. As stated, Ayla's classroom teachers also created another video to help Ayla learn to state that she is "all done" with an activity instead of throwing the materials.

## ARTIE (FOUR YEARS OLD): SENSORY PLAY
### Child background

Artie, a four-year-old boy with ASD, received special education services through his school district within a special education preschool classroom. Artie also received a variety of private therapies outside of his school day including occupational therapy, speech therapy, vision therapy, listening therapy, and verbal behavior therapy. Artie had a large vocabulary but struggled with using his language socially. He primarily used language to obtain items or activities. He used one-word labels and familiar carrier phrases such as, "I want____, please," to get what he wanted. Imitation of others was difficult for Artie. When regulated and when no distractions were present, Artie imitated a three-step series of actions such as first clapping, then touching his head, and then stomping his feet, particularly when the actions were paired with animated expression or silly verbalization by the adult. He also imitated simple actions with objects such as tapping rhythm sticks, stacking blocks, and shaking a maraca. It became extremely difficult for Artie to imitate actions when favorite items, including sensory media, were present in the room. When playing with sensory media such as finger paint, rice, sand, or play dough, Artie became immersed in the sensory experience and was unable to attend to or imitate the actions of others. His independent play with sensory media in a sensory table included rubbing the material between his fingertips and flicking the material in the air. Artie did not use tools such as shovels, buckets, or mills. Even with hand-over-hand assistance, Artie would go back to rubbing and flicking the sensory materials as soon as the adult support was removed.

## Description of the video

A PVM video was created to help Artie increase his functional use of tools with sensory media on the sensory table. Before the video was made, the sensory table was filled with rice, one shovel, one scoop, one bucket, and one mill. In the video, the actions of scooping and dumping were modeled with the materials. Artie's teacher was the actor in this video. The teacher's aide held the video camera next to the teacher's head and only filmed the teacher's hands. In the first segment, the scoop was used to scoop rice and dump it into the mill. This action was repeated four times. In the second segment, the shovel was used to scoop rice and dump it in the bucket. This action was also repeated four times. The video began with the actor saying, "Time to play sensory table." Throughout the video, the actor labeled the actions such as, "Scoop," "Dump," "Get shovel," and "All done scoop." The video ended with the actor saying, "All done sensory table." This video was one-and-a-half minutes long and did not require editing.

## Viewing the video

The video was saved on a laptop computer that was used in Artie's classroom for video modeling purposes. The laptop was placed on a small table next to the sensory table. Before Artie played at the sensory table, he sat with an adult and watched the video. He seemed interested in the video as he repeatedly looked from the video to the sensory table, but always returned his attention to the video. After watching the video, the adult told Artie, "Artie's turn. Time for sensory table."

## Facilitating skill development following the video

The first two times that Artie played at the sensory table after watching the video, he immediately began rubbing the rice between his fingers and flicking it in the air. The adult physically helped Artie to use the tools and modeled the language used in the video, "Scoop and dump." The adult also directed Artie to use the different tools by stating, "All done shovel. Get scoop." On the third day that Artie watched the video, he independently picked up the scoop and began to scoop rice. With physical support, he then dumped the rice into the mill. Over the course of the next three school days, Artie became more independent in using the tools for both scooping and dumping; however, he often dropped the tools after two to three turns in order to rub the rice between his fingers. Verbal or physical prompts were then necessary for Artie to again pick up a tool and begin scooping. Since it was such a strong desire for Artie to touch the rice with his hands, it was decided that he should be given an opportunity for self-directed play prior to demonstrating the actions in the video. The hope was that, given the opportunity to play with the materials as he wanted for a brief period, Artie would then be able to use the tools more functionally. The revised video watching and play sequence was as follows: (1) Artie watched the video; (2) Artie was given the opportunity to play with the rice using his hands for a verbal count of ten seconds; (3) Artie was given the verbal prompt, "Time to scoop;" and (4) Artie then used the tools for ten scoops.

## Child outcomes

After watching the video for two more days with the revised video watching and play sequence, Artie was able to use both the shovel and the scoop to dump rice into the mill and the bucket for ten scoops. Although in the video the scoop was always used with the mill and the shovel was used with the bucket, Artie used the scooping tools interchangeably with both receptacles. Artie's time at the sensory table became more functional; he engaged in less rubbing and flicking and used the tools appropriately.

## Fading and generalization

Artie continued to watch the video each day before playing at the sensory table. The classroom staff continued to see an increase in his functional play skills. Artie demonstrated these skills even as the rice was substituted with other dry sensory media, such as flax seed or sand, and the scooping tools were substituted with other similar scooping tools. The rice PVM video was not effective when the sensory table contained water as Artie was not able to generalize his skills to water play. A different PVM video for water play was created. The original "rice" video was systematically faded from use within the classroom over a period of two weeks. Artie has also demonstrated generalization of his scooping and dumping skills when playing in the playground without watching the video. When Artie was flicking the sand in the playground and an adult handed him a shovel and bucket saying, "Time to scoop," Artie began using the shovel to fill the bucket.

# KOOPER (FIVE YEARS OLD):
# CLEANING UP TOYS
## Child background

Kooper, a five-year-old boy with ASD, received in-center special education services through his school district. He had attended a preschool classroom for the past three years in which he received services from a special education teacher, a speech and language pathologist, and an autism specialist. Kooper demonstrated many skills commensurate to a child of his same age including an age-typical vocabulary. His services mainly addressed his challenges with social communication and perspective taking. Kooper often developed nonproductive patterns in his behavior. One of these patterns related to clean-up time within his preschool classroom. When the teacher signaled that it was time to clean up, Kooper left the play area he was in and ran across the classroom. While the other children were putting toys away, Kooper would walk around the room and not help put toys away. His teacher had tried a variety of strategies to encourage Kooper to participate in clean-up including social stories, visuals, reward charts, and peer modeling. Despite these strategies, Kooper continued to require heavy adult support in order to clean up. Often when verbally prompted to clean up, Kooper would yell loudly that he didn't want to clean.

## Description of the video

A PVM video was created to interrupt Kooper's behavior pattern and to teach him the skills needed to participate in the clean-up routine. When class was not in session, Kooper's favorite train set was arranged in the toy area of his classroom. Two adults were necessary in making this video. Kooper's special education teacher was the actor and the person who held the camera. Kooper's general education preschool teacher played herself in the video. The special education teacher held the camera next to her own face and recorded her free hand. In the video, the special education teacher's hands were shown playing with the train set. The preschool teacher then called out to the class, "Boys and girls, one more minute until clean-up time." When the preschool teacher said, "Boys and girls," the camera shifted to look up at her. When the announcement was done, the camera shifted back to the actor's hands playing with the trains. In one minute, the teacher played the notes on a xylophone as her signal for clean-up time. The camera then shifted from the train to the teacher. The teacher then announced, "Boys and girls, it's time to put the toys away," and sang the class clean-up song. The camera shifted back to the train set to show the actor's hands putting pieces of the train set into a toy bin. As each piece was put in the toy bin, the actor counted. It was thought that giving Kooper a set number of items to put away would be helpful. The actor put away 15 items and then placed the toy bin onto the toy shelf. The actor/person holding the camera then walked toward the sink to show washing hands for a snack, the next activity in the class schedule. It is important to note that throughout this video, the camera shows the actions from Kooper's perspective. This video did not require any editing as it was filmed in one continuous session with all of the verbal directions recorded during the video shoot.

## Viewing the video

The video was saved onto the classroom laptop. Toward the end of play time, the video was shown to Kooper while he was playing with the train set. Many of Kooper's peers were interested in the video and watched it with him. The first time Kooper and his peers watched the video, they were very interested in pointing out the familiar items in the movie, such as, "Hey, that's our train and that's our toy shelf. There's our teacher!" Kooper and his peers returned to playing until the teacher gave the one-minute warning. At this time, Kooper paused in his play to shift his attention to the teacher. He then turned to the special education teacher and said, "It's just like the movie!"

## Facilitating skill development following the video

The video was immediately successful. When the teacher announced that it was time to clean up, many of the children, including Kooper, began putting toys away and counting out the items up to 15. After Kooper put 15 items away, he turned to an adult and asked, "Now what? I can't remember." He was directed toward the sink to wash his hands. The video was shown every day near the end of play time. So many of Kooper's classmates were interested in watching the video that it was decided that it would be shown on the large interactive whiteboard on the classroom wall instead of on the laptop.

## Child outcomes

The video was judged a complete success. No modifications to the video were needed. Not only did Kooper immediately begin participating in the clean-up routine, many of his classmates became more active participants as well.

## Fading and generalization

The video was used for the remainder of the school year. Each day during play time, one of Kooper's peers would invariably request to watch the video on the interactive whiteboard. There were a few days that the video was not shown due to a change in the schedule or some other obstacle. On these days, Kooper did very well cleaning up. He put away 15 items and washed his hands for a snack. It was originally a concern that Kooper would only put away the train set because that is what the video portrayed; this was never an issue. Kooper generalized this skill and always put away the toys in the area where he was playing whenever he heard the xylophone and the teacher saying it was clean-up time. Kooper's mother requested to have a copy of the video for use at home. The video was burned to a DVD so Kooper could watch it on the family television. Kooper did not respond well to watching the video at home. He told his mother that the movie was for school, not home. It was determined that a different video would be filmed at home for home use.

# 4

# REVIEW OF CURRENT RESEARCH ON VIDEO MODELING

It may not be widely known to the general population, but US law requires public school teachers to use evidence-based practice in their classrooms. This involves teaching methods that have been thoroughly tested and proven to be effective in peer-reviewed research. Two of the most significant federal education policies, the No Child Left Behind Act of 2001 and the Individuals with Disabilities Education Act (IDEA) of 2004, require the use of evidence-based practice in schools to improve the learning outcomes for all students. Because of this legislated requirement and because educators and parents want to use the most effective treatments and strategies, it is important to be well versed in the most recent research.

The National Professional Development Center on Autism Spectrum Disorders (NPDC on ASD) is a multi-university center in North America that promotes the use of evidence-based practice for those with autism spectrum disorder (ASD) at ages birth through 21 years. According to the NPDC on ASD, video modeling is evidence-based practice, and those who work with individuals with ASD should be encouraged to use it (Video Modeling: Overview 2010). The majority of the video modeling research conducted thus far has focused on Basic Video Modeling (BVM), but there is a base of research concentrating on Video Self-Modeling (VSM) and Point-of-view Video Modeling (PVM) that has led the NPDC on ASD to identify *all* three types of video modeling as evidence-based practice. Our hope is that this review of research will inform readers of the effectiveness of the various types of video modeling as well as the wide variety of skills and routines that can be addressed through video modeling.

The following 11 studies are arranged by the type of video modeling used as well as by the skill or routine targeted. These studies were chosen based on the type of video modeling used as well as the young ages and developmental needs of the subjects (most had a diagnosis of ASD). This should not be considered a comprehensive review of all research on video modeling.

# BASIC VIDEO MODELING
## Perspective taking

In 2003, Charlop-Christy and Daneshvar studied the effectiveness of teaching basic perspective-taking skills to a group of young boys using BVM. Perspective taking refers to the ability to determine mental states of others in order to explain or predict behavior. In typically developing children, this skill appears around the age of four (Baron-Cohen, Leslie, and Frith 1985). In their landmark study, Baron-Cohen, Leslie, and Firth conducted the now-famous Sally–Anne task to test children's understanding of false beliefs, a task that requires perspective-taking skills. In the Sally–Anne task, children were shown two puppets (Sally and Anne), a basket, a box, and a marble. Sally put the marble in the basket and left the room. Anne then moved the marble to the box. When Sally returned to the room, the experimenter asked each child where Sally would look for the marble. The correct answer was, of course, that Sally would look in the basket. If the children answered correctly, it showed that they understood Sally's perspective, that Sally falsely believed the marble was in the basket. If the children answered incorrectly, it demonstrated that the children were not able to take Sally's perspective, therefore answering the question based on their own information, not Sally's information. Baron-Cohen *et al.* found that perspective taking is delayed or absent in children with ASD.

In the Charlop-Christy and Daneshvar study, three boys (two aged six and one aged nine) were taught perspective-taking skills using BVM. The boys were shown BVM videos of adults performing perspective-taking, false belief tasks similar to the Sally–Anne task. Within the videos, the adults also explained their thought processes of figuring out the correct answers; basically, how they figured out what another person's perspective was. After watching the videos, the boys were then asked questions similar to the Sally–Anne task question, "Where will Sally look for the marble?" After watching the videos, the boys were given tasks to complete that would demonstrate their understanding of false beliefs. All three boys quickly demonstrated an increase in perspective-taking skills that they maintained over time. Additionally, two of the boys generalized their perspective-taking skills to untrained tasks.

## Sociodramatic play in a group

In 2012, Ozen, Batu, and Birkan looked at the effectiveness of using BVM to teach sociodramatic play to three nine-year-old boys with ASD. BVM videos were created to teach three play scenarios, each containing three separate roles: canteen (cashier, customer, and canteen worker), school (teacher, student, and inspector), and hospital (doctor, nurse, and patient.) Each play scenario was quite detailed and lengthy. There were between 14 and 20 steps for each role within each play scenario. The same three adults played the roles in each video. The training sessions took place once a week for 48 weeks. Each boy was assigned a role in each scene. During each session, the boys watched the BVM video of the play scenario and acted out the scene. Results of the study showed that BVM was effective in teaching sociodramatic play skills in a small group. Two weeks after the study ended, the boys had maintained their new play skills. During observation sessions, the researchers noted that the boys had also learned the roles of their partners.

## Social language

In this study, Maione and Mirenda (2006) examined the effectiveness of using BVM to teach a five-year-old boy with ASD to use social language with community peers during play. BVM videos were created using play materials that were interesting to the child including modeling dough, toy cars, and a playground toy set with figurines. In the videos, two adults were filmed demonstrating the following social language skills: commenting, questioning, acknowledging, initiating, responding, and other language behaviors. In his home, the boy watched each BVM video one time every day and engaged in two to three 15-minute play sessions with two peers each week. Video feedback, verbal prompts, and a visual prompt were added to five of the sessions to help increase the verbalizations during the toy car play activities because the boy was not increasing his utterances. The video feedback and prompts were only used within the toy car play activities and were withdrawn after five play sessions when the child's rate of verbalizations increased and remained stable. Results showed that BVM was effective in teaching social language with peers during play activities. Both scripted and unscripted language increased. Positive changes were measured for both responding and initiating, particularly initiating. The study also demonstrated that unfamiliar adults could be used successfully as models within BVM videos.

## Picture Exchange Communication System (PECS)

In 2012, Cihak, Smith, Cornett, and Coleman evaluated the use of BVM in conjunction with the Picture Exchange Communication System (PECS) to increase communicative initiations with preschoolers with ASD and developmental delays. With PECS, children use pictures as tools to communicate. Four three-year-old children with limited communication skills participated. The children attended preschool classes designed for typically developing peers as well as a special education preschool class. The training sessions took place in both types of classrooms. BVM videos were created of a peer model using PECS during snack time, center time, and play time with a teacher. The children received either PECS-only instruction or watched a BVM video prior to PECS. The children watched the videos on a laptop computer in the same natural environment as the upcoming PECS activity. All the children learned to use PECS and increased their communicative initiations; however, the children who watched the BVM videos learned to use PECS more quickly.

## Perception of emotion

In this study completed in 2003, Corbett focused on the effectiveness of improving one child's ability to perceive the emotional states of others using BVM. The child was presented with a series of BVM videos depicting children playing and interacting with others while demonstrating four basic emotions: happy, sad, angry, and afraid. The results showed that BVM was an effective tool for the attainment and generalization of emotion perception in this child with ASD.

## Representational play

In 2003, D'Ateno, Mangiapanello, and Taylor completed a study that examined the effectiveness of teaching imaginary play sequences using BVM. The subjects in this study were preschool children with ASD. The children watched BVM videos of relatively long, representational play sequences including physical actions and verbalizations. The three play scenarios depicted in the BVM videos included having a tea party, shopping, and baking. The results indicated that BVM led to the rapid acquisition of both verbal and physical play responses for all three play sequences.

# VIDEO SELF-MODELING
## Making requests

In 1996, Hepting and Goldstein completed a study that examined the effectiveness of using VSM to teach young children to make spontaneous requests and to generalize this skill across classroom activities. Four preschool children with developmental delays participated. VSM videos were created showing the children independently and appropriately requesting items during snack time and play time. With additional prompting and praise, the children learned to request items within their preschool classroom.

VSM was determined to be an effective teaching strategy to increase the requesting skills in preschoolers.

## Decreasing pushing, increasing verbal responding, and increasing conversation initiation

In 2005, Buggey completed a study involving a preschool boy with ASD who was demonstrating aggressive behavior. Buggey created a VSM video in order to decrease the boy's aggressive behavior of pushing, while also increasing verbal responding and conversation initiations. In the video, the boy was depicted interacting positively with peers and using appropriate touch. The video also contained edited interactions depicting the child verbally interacting with peers (both initiations and responses). After watching the VSM video, the boy's pushing behavior ceased and his responses to peers' questions increased significantly. Initially, the boy did not make progress in initiating conversations. However, Buggey re-edited the video to show the boy verbally initiating with peers as opposed to responding to peers' questions. Buggey felt that the back-and-forth exchanges in the video might have been distracting to the boy. After the boy viewed the re-edited video, his level of initiations also increased.

### Peer initiations

Buggey, *et al.* (2011) examined the effectiveness of VSM at increasing the social initiations in preschool children with ASD during playground play. Separate VSM videos were created for four children. Each video was edited to show the target child initiating interactions with a peer and then the two children playing together in the playground. Each child watched his video an hour prior to outdoor recess. The videos were shown to the children ten times within a two-week period, and were then withdrawn. The results were mostly positive, with two children exhibiting major treatment effects, one with questionable results, and one child being unaffected.

## Peer interactions

In 2007, Bellini, Akullian, and Hopf completed a study that examined the effectiveness of VSM at increasing the social engagement in young children with ASD. Their study expanded upon a previous study on VSM by measuring social interactions with same-aged peers in a natural setting rather than with adults in a controlled clinical setting. The researchers worked with two preschool children with ASD. They created videos showing the children interacting verbally and physically with community peers. Both children demonstrated large improvements in their peer interactions, both in quantity and in quality.

# POINT-OF-VIEW VIDEO MODELING

## Play skills

In 2006, Hine and Wolery evaluated the effectiveness of PVM in teaching toy play actions to two preschoolers with autism. The researchers studied the children's acquisition and maintenance of play actions. They also studied the degree to which the preschoolers used the new skills when playing with novel toys and during classroom activities. The results indicated that PVM is an effective tool for teaching toy play actions to preschoolers with ASD.

## Social skills

In 2010, Tretreault and Lerman investigated the use of PVM to teach three children with ASD (ages four, five, and eight) to initiate and maintain conversations with adults. They specifically targeted increasing eye contact, initiating verbalizations, and responding to verbalizations. During treatment, the researchers used food to reinforce the target behaviors in addition to using the PVM videos. Three different PVM videos were created. The videos illustrated different play situations with scripted exchanges that would elicit one of the four targeted verbalizations from the child (showing a creation with a verbalization, asking for help, sharing a toy on request, and verbally requesting a turn). The training sessions were conducted in a small therapy room with an adult as the play partner. Each child watched a PVM video and was then immediately invited to play with the adult using the same materials that were used in the video. The children were measured on their ability to engage in the scripted exchanges depicted in the videos as well as their ability to make eye contact during these exchanges.

Results showed that PVM was successful in teaching the verbal scripts to the three children with varying amounts of food reinforcers and prompts. The results were as follows. Child One was given food as a reinforcer for attending to the video and for initiating verbalizations. He learned all three scripts and increased his eye contact. Child Two was also given food as a reinforcer for attending to the video and for initiating verbalizations. He learned two out of three scripts and increased his eye contact. Child Three was not given a food reinforcer for attending to the video but was given food for initiating verbalizations. Gestural and partial verbal prompts were needed for Child Three to learn to initiate verbalizations and to increase eye contact. For all three children, eye contact was acquired and maintained more often than scripted vocal behavior. Tretreault and Lerman questioned the necessity of using arbitrary food reinforcers in conjunction with VSM. They also felt that further research was needed in order to investigate the effectiveness of using PVM in teaching social behavior.

We hope that this review of research gives some indication of the great possibilities that video modeling provides for parents and professionals who work with young children with ASD. Although there is not a huge wealth of research supporting the use of video modeling (relative to other evidence-based practice), what is available is extremely positive. This technique has been shown, both anecdotally and within research studies, to be effective at teaching a wide variety of skills in all areas of development in the home, school, and community. We believe there is enough evidence to point toward video modeling earning its place as a conventional, mainstream teaching strategy for young children with ASD.

CHAPTER

# 5

# OTHER USES OF
# VIDEO-RECORDING DEVICES

Basic Video Modeling (BVM), Video Self-Modeling (VSM), and Point-of-view Video Modeling (PVM) are only a few of the ways you can use a video-recording device to help support the development of young children with autism spectrum disorders (ASD). In this chapter, we describe several other ways in which we put our video-recording devices to good use in children's homes, in the classroom, or out in the community. The topics we cover include reflective practices, adult training, progress monitoring, and lesson extension activities.

## REFLECTIVE PRACTICES

Reflective practice is the ability to reflect your own actions in order to learn from your everyday experiences (Schön 1983). As professionals in any field, we are taught to be reflective in order to get the most out of our daily experiences in the workplace. Just like more formal types of training completed during workshops, professional conferences, and college courses, sitting back and reflecting upon each day's proceedings is an effective way to strengthen your ability to produce high quality work.

# Reflective practices for adults

When engaged in routines with young children with ASD (whether as a caregiver or a service provider), it is often difficult to immediately determine the cause of each observed behavior. Remember that behavior refers to everything your child does, not just the naughty stuff. Some puzzling behaviors that you may observe during a routine may be a lack of eye contact, limited participation, or physical aggression such as hitting or biting. Because you may not be sure why the behavior is occurring, it is extremely difficult to determine an effective response, especially when you are "in the moment." Being reflective on these situations is often helpful in determining a plan for next time. However, there are many instances in which you may not have caught all of the important information surrounding the situation in question, such as your possible lack of facial expressions, your possible excessive physical support, or the noise of other children playing in the background. When important information is overlooked, reflecting upon the routine may not give you the answers you need. Here is where video-recording devices come into play. If you are able to record the routine during which the confusing behavior is occurring, you will now have an excellent visual support to aide you in your reflection. Recording yourself participating a routine with the child and then later reviewing the raw footage is an excellent way to increase your awareness of how you are interacting with the child. It is also a great way to determine what accommodations need to be made in order for the child to be more successful completing that routine in that particular environment.

Reflective practices are valuable to all of those who work with young children with ASD. If you are a primary caregiver, you can start by recording yourself completing a routine with your child. We suggest that you start with a routine that you would like to change in some way. If there is no one around to operate the camera, remember that a tripod will often do the trick. Before reviewing the video footage, reflect upon all of the strategies that are helpful in facilitating your child's development. Some of these strategies may include following through with consistent steps within the routine, using simple language, exaggerating your facial expressions, pausing for eye contact, using visual supports, providing sensory input, etc. While viewing the video footage, keep your eye open for these helpful strategies as well as how your child responds. If you observe your child demonstrating any unexpected behaviors during the routine, it will be important for you to determine a possible source of the unexpected behaviors. We often refer to the source of a behavior as the antecedent. Examine the video footage immediately prior to the behavior in question to determine what the potential antecedent might be. Watch for how you responded to this behavior and try to identify other possible responses that might be more effective. Study the environment to determine if there are any accommodations that could be made. Accommodations may include decreased clutter on the walls and shelves, a different type of chair that better supports your child, noise-canceling headphones to drown out all background noise, etc.

If you are a service provider (e.g., early intervention teacher, special education teacher, speech and language pathologist), you can also use video-recording devices in order to capture video footage to be used in reflection. Watching yourself in action can be a powerful tool that often elicits an imperative change in the way you teach young children with ASD. Engaging in reflective practices with the support of video footage on a regular basis has the power to transform you into a more mindful and effective professional.

## Reflective practices for young children with ASD
### Self-awareness

As mentioned in the introduction to this book, children with ASD are often not aware of their own behaviors and how their behaviors may be affecting those around them such as their caregivers, siblings, peers, etc. In order to increase the self-awareness skills in a child with ASD, begin by recording the child engaging in a routine in which an unexpected behavior often occurs. As discussed in Chapter 1, an "unexpected behavior" refers to any behavior that is socially inappropriate. In a quiet and minimally distracting environment, have the child watch the unedited, raw video footage. This footage can be viewed on the video-recording device itself, although we find it more useful to show the video on a larger screen such as a computer screen, television, or interactive whiteboard. Pause the video immediately following the child's unexpected behavior in order to highlight the reactions of those around him. The video clip can be replayed multiple times in order for the child to observe, label, and discuss the feelings of those around him. We often find it helpful to engage in Social Behavior Mapping (SBM) at this time. SBM is a visual strategy developed by Michelle Garcia Winner to help any individual with ASD understand that each behavior he demonstrates (whether expected or unexpected) influences how other people think and feel about him (2007). These thoughts and emotions have an impact on each person's response to the child's behavior. These responses to the child's behavior will, in turn, affect the emotional state of the individual with ASD. See Figure 5.1 for an example of a Social Behavior Map that we used to increase self-awareness in a four-year-old boy with ASD.

| When you... | Your teacher feels... | What happens? | You feel... |
|---|---|---|---|
| Use gentle hands | Happy | You get to keep playing | Happy |
| Hit a friend | Angry | You are all done playing | Sad or mad |

Figure 5.1. An example of a Social Behavior Map

A Social Behavior Map can serve as a visual reminder in the future regarding what unexpected behavior the child displayed, how it made others feel, what the child's consequence was, and how that made the child feel in return. For example, if one was created to explain the effects of yelling out during circle time, this static visual can be reviewed with the child immediately prior to each circle time and can serve as a visual prompt to the child during circle time in the hope of decreasing his unexpected behaviors.

In addition to focusing on unexpected behaviors, we believe that it is equally important to complete the sequence of recording, video review and discussion, and SBM to increase the child's awareness of his expected behaviors and how those behaviors can have a positive impact on others. As explained in Chapter 1, expected behaviors are those that are socially appropriate. This process will often serve as a proactive behavior management strategy, which may decrease the amount of unexpected behaviors demonstrated by the child. Please note that while SBM is a strategy that can be extremely helpful in increasing a child's awareness of his behaviors and how they affect others, it is not imperative to increasing a child's self-awareness skills.

We have found that this type of reflective practice will not be beneficial to all young children with ASD. In order for the child to benefit from viewing unedited video footage of himself in action and engaging in discussions regarding how his behaviors affect others, he needs to demonstrate a certain level of cognitive, language, and social/emotional functioning. In addition, each child with ASD will respond differently to watching a video clip of himself engaged in a routine. While viewing themselves demonstrating expected behaviors would be beneficial to most children with ASD, it may be a different story when it comes to viewing themselves demonstrating unexpected behaviors. In some situations, the act of viewing the unexpected behavior can actually serve as VSM for the child, which will increase the occurrence of that unexpected behavior in the future. This could occur if the child does not understand that he should not copy what he sees, but rather use the video footage to determine how his behaviors are affecting others. If you are unaware of whether or not the child is at the level needed in order to participate in and understand the discussions that take place during the unedited, raw video footage viewing, we suggest that you tread lightly.

## Self-monitoring

Video-recording devices can also play a major role in teaching young children with ASD to monitor their own behaviors. Self-monitoring goes beyond the basic awareness of behaviors and involves the child observing, identifying, and recording the frequency of his own behaviors. The ability for a young child with ASD to self-monitor his own behavior becomes increasingly important as he transitions into less restrictive classrooms, therefore receiving less adult support. Self-monitoring strategies have been successful at reducing stereotypic behaviors (e.g., body rocking, hand flapping), and increasing functional play, independence during daily routines, and on task behavior (Hume, Loftin, and Lantz 2009). We believe that self-monitoring is an important skill to begin teaching before children start elementary school. Below are four steps that we suggest following when beginning to teach children with ASD how to monitor their own behaviors:

1. Videotape a routine in which the child is demonstrating high frequencies of an expected behavior. For example, if the child does a nice job of responding to his name when called during play, play time would be a good routine to record.

2. Define the target behavior to the child. For example, if you would like the child to monitor his ability to respond to his name when called, you will need to make sure that the child knows exactly what it looks like when he appropriately responds to his name being called. This step will look different for each child. You might find it helpful to define the target behavior using pictures, video, role-playing, etc.

3. Explain to the child how you would like him to respond when he observes the target behavior. This could include raising his hand, pushing a buzzer, placing a popsicle stick in a cup, etc.

4. Allow the child to watch the unedited, raw video footage. While viewing, only reinforce the child for his ability to

respond correctly when he observes the target behavior (e.g., raising his hand when he observes himself appropriately responding to his name being called). Do not reinforce him for any behaviors displayed in the video.

Once the child is able to accurately monitor a few of his own expected behaviors, complete steps one through four in regards to unexpected behaviors.

# ADULT TRAINING

Video-recording devices are useful tools when training a variety of adults on how to effectively interact with young children with ASD. If you are an early intervention or special education service provider who provides routines-based intervention within children's homes or community settings, your role during therapy sessions is to train caregivers how to effectively use strategies to target an increase in their child's skills during naturally occurring routines.

If used properly, video-recording devices have the power to enhance caregiver training within routines-based intervention. During each therapy session (e.g., home visit), we suggest prompting the caregiver to choose a routine that they would like to work on with her child. As the caregiver and child complete the routine, record it from start to finish. Routines to record may include anything from book reading or play with toys to snack or bath time. The recording should capture both the adult and the child as they work through the routine or activity together. The same footage that was recorded in order for caregivers to reflect upon their interactions with their child (as described in the "Reflective practices for adults" section of this chapter, see pp.116–17) can also be used for training purposes. After recording the routine, we find it helpful to sit down with the child's caregiver and review the raw video footage together. During your review, you can pause the video in order to reinforce the caregiver for following through with a specific strategy, discuss how the child responded to the strategy, problem solve ways to decrease or increase the occurrence of specific behaviors, etc. We understand that this type of training can be completed without the use of a video-recording device, just by simply discussing the routine immediately after it was completed. However, we feel that caregivers are able to gain more understanding regarding what their child needs and how they can best support their child when these discussions are supported by video. Additionally, the use of video during this type of training allows caregivers to learn in a less distracting environment because their child does not need to be present (for the reason that the routine was completed and recorded at an earlier time, thus the training can take place while the child is watching a video, napping, at school, etc.).

Routines-based intervention is a service delivery model that meets all regulations set forth by the Individuals With Disabilities Education Improvement Act (IDEIA) of 2004. The IDEIA, also known as Public Law 108-446, requires that all infants and toddlers with disabilities receive their early intervention services in the most natural environments, which is typically their home. The IDEIA 2004 also requires that early intervention services include "family training, counseling and home visits." As stated earlier, routines-based intervention involves the service provider training the caregiver (rather than working directly with the child) to target an increase in their child's skills across naturally occurring routines. This type of intervention is typically more meaningful to young children because the "therapy" is embedded into familiar routines, which occur in familiar places with familiar people. Routines-based intervention provides an opportunity for the following to occur: (1) increased generalization of skills because deficits are being addressed across the child's day, which most likely involves a variety of play partners and settings (e.g., home, playground, grocery store); (2) increased maintenance of skills because the strategies introduced to the caregivers are easily incorporated into their daily routines and soon become a new and natural way of interacting with the child, which creates an opportunity for ongoing treatment; and (3) increased hours of early intervention services given that the child's deficits can be addressed at home by the caregivers and not just during short in-center therapy sessions or during weekly home visits (Mahoney and Perales 2003; Schertz and Odom 2007; Wetherby and Woods 2006). Routines-based intervention allows children to receive at least 25 hours of active engagement each week, which is what the National Research Council recommends for young children with ASD (Lord and McGee 2001).

It is not uncommon for a child with ASD to perform better with one caregiver than he does with another. In order to figure out why this may be occurring, it can be very helpful to videotape the same routine twice; once with the caregiver with whom the child performs well and once with the caregiver with whom the child performs poorly. If you are a service provider, we suggest that you sit down and review this video footage with caregivers in order to help them determine a reason for the child's inconsistencies. Once this is determined, the video footage of the child performing well can be used to train other caregivers on how to best facilitate their child's skills during that routine.

We all know how important consistency is for a young child with ASD; however, it is not always easy to provide this consistency when a child has a variety of caregivers, teachers, therapists, etc. Before we started using video-recording devices, it was necessary to spend several hours each week collaborating with other programs and their staff through email, phone conversations, and face-to-face meetings to provide the needed information so that all of the adults in the child's life were "on the same page." Now, with the use of video, we are able to ensure greater consistency for each child across programs, environments, caregivers, and service providers. If you, too, struggle with making certain that a child with ASD receives consistent services (whether you are a service provider or a caregiver), you might find it helpful to coordinate the child's services through the use of video. We suggest starting by videotaping *all* supports and strategies in use, which might include specific activities completed by the child as well as precise techniques used by certain adults. Specific activities completed by the child may include the use of a picture schedule to manage transitions or a work system in order to organize a specific routine. Techniques used by adults that would be helpful to record include the use of nonverbal prompting during a routine, the use of a visual in order to proactively manage a particular behavior, or a hands-on approach used to aid a child in calming down. If the child uses individualized visual supports that may not be self-explanatory, we suggest having someone videotape you going through each visual in detail in order to explain why, when, and how it should be used. Remember, you can use a tripod if no one is available to operate the camera. Once the clips have been recorded, save them onto a USB flash drive. This flash drive can be shared with all those who interact with the child.

## PROGRESS MONITORING

Monitoring a child's progress toward the mastery of a certain skill is sometimes easier said than done. Some skills are easier to observe and record than others. For example, while it may be easy to observe and immediately document a child's ability to correctly respond to a verbal direction, the same might not true for behaviors such as referencing a social partner or coordinating eye gaze with gestures. If you find yourself struggling to record accurate data, try using your video-recording device by recording the child for short periods of time across a variety of routines. This video footage can then be analyzed in order to obtain accurate information regarding the child's exact level of functioning. Video-recording devices are also a great way to illustrate progress to a variety of caregivers. As services providers, we are accustomed to looking at a child's progress in terms of numbers on paper. As caregivers, it is often more beneficial for them to review video clips from across time in order to get a true picture of what progress their child has made.

## LESSON EXTENSION ACTIVITIES

Because many children with ASD often benefit from repeated exposure to the same adult-directed, group learning activity, we find it helpful to use video-recording devices in order to bring some excitement to our classroom as well as to reinforce important cognitive and language-based skills in a more motivating way. This added excitement is almost always a sure way to increase each child's motivation and attention toward an old and possibly boring (yet very important!) activity. After reading the same story or singing the same song for a few days in a row, bring your video-recording device to class and record the children acting out the story or song. The children don't necessarily need to be able to act out the entire story or song from beginning to end. If you are comfortable with editing, the recording process will be very easy because you can record the story or song in small segments. Once the filming has been completed, splice the raw video footage so that the story or song progresses smoothly from start to finish. On the next day, instead of just reading the story or singing the song, you can have your students watch themselves on-screen as they bring the story or song to life! The process of acting out the story or song and then later watching the completed video not only increases our students' interest in the activity, but it also increases their ability to complete a variety of other cognitive and language tasks. Some of the specific skills that we have observed to increase following this process include the ability to participate in motor movements associated with familiar songs, recall information, answer yes/no questions, answer Wh-questions (i.e., who, what, where, when), sequence visual information describing a familiar story, and retell a familiar story.

# WHICH TYPE OF VIDEO MODELING SHOULD I USE?

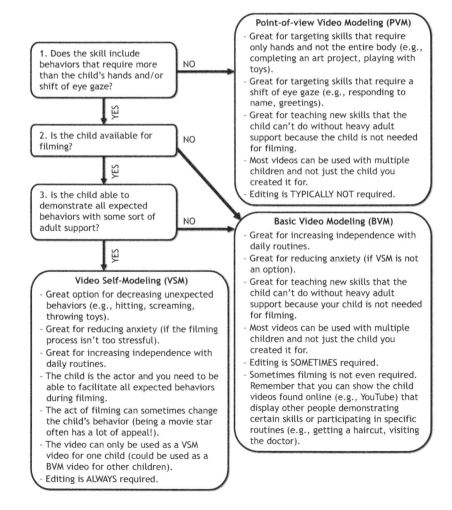

**Point-of-view Video Modeling (PVM)**
- Great for targeting skills that require only hands and not the entire body (e.g., completing an art project, playing with toys).
- Great for targeting skills that require a shift of eye gaze (e.g., responding to name, greetings).
- Great for teaching new skills that the child can't do without heavy adult support because the child is not needed for filming.
- Most videos can be used with multiple children and not just the child you created it for.
- Editing is TYPICALLY NOT required.

1. Does the skill include behaviors that require more than the child's hands and/or shift of eye gaze?

NO / YES

2. Is the child available for filming?

NO / YES

3. Is the child able to demonstrate all expected behaviors with some sort of adult support?

NO / YES

**Basic Video Modeling (BVM)**
- Great for increasing independence with daily routines.
- Great for reducing anxiety (if VSM is not an option).
- Great for teaching new skills that the child can't do without heavy adult support because your child is not needed for filming.
- Most videos can be used with multiple children and not just the child you created it for.
- Editing is SOMETIMES required.
- Sometimes filming is not even required. Remember that you can show the child videos found online (e.g., YouTube) that display other people demonstrating certain skills or participating in specific routines (e.g., getting a haircut, visiting the doctor).

**Video Self-Modeling (VSM)**
- Great option for decreasing unexpected behaviors (e.g., hitting, screaming, throwing toys).
- Great for reducing anxiety (if the filming process isn't too stressful).
- Great for increasing independence with daily routines.
- The child is the actor and you need to be able to facilitate all expected behaviors during filming.
- The act of filming can sometimes change the child's behavior (being a movie star often has a lot of appeal!).
- The video can only be used as a VSM video for one child (could be used as a BVM video for other children).
- Editing is ALWAYS required.

# Appendix B
# SAMPLE OUTLINES FOR PLANNING AND CREATING VIDEOS

| SKILL: |
| --- |
| |

| TARGETED BEHAVIORS: |
| --- |
| |

| VIDEO TYPE: | LOCATION: |
| --- | --- |

| MATERIALS NEEDED: | PEOPLE NEEDED:<br>  Recorder:<br>  Actor(s): |
| --- | --- |

| CAMERA LOCATION and FOCUS: |
| --- |
| |

| Action | Scripted language |
| --- | --- |
| | |
| | |
| | |
| | |
| | |
| | |
| | |
| | |
| | |
| | |
| | |
| | |

*Figure B.1. Reproducible outline template*

**SKILL:**
Washing hands

**TARGETED BEHAVIORS:**
- Stepping up to the sink
- Turning on the faucet
- Getting hands wet
- Getting soap
- Rubbing hands for 20 seconds while singing song
- Rinsing hands
- Turning off the faucet
- Drying hands
- Throwing away paper towel

| VIDEO TYPE:<br>Basic Video Modeling (BVM) | LOCATION:<br>Sink |
|---|---|
| **MATERIALS NEEDED:**<br>-Sink -Stool -Paper towel<br>-Soap -Video camera -Trash can | **PEOPLE NEEDED:**<br>Recorder: Sarah<br>Actor(s): Brenna |

**CAMERA LOCATION and FOCUS:**
Sarah will focus the camera on Brenna's hands and the materials (sink, faucet, soap, paper towel, trash can).

| Action | Scripted language |
|---|---|
| Step up to the sink | "Time to wash hands." |
| Turn on the faucet | "Turn on water." |
| Get hands wet | "Get hands wet." |
| Get soap | "Get soap." |
| Rub hands together including tops, bottoms, and in between fingers. | "Wash hands." Sing the hand washing song. |
| Rinse hands under the running water. | "Rinse hands. Get off all the bubbles." |
| Turn off faucet. | "Turn off water." |
| Get a paper towel. | "Get towel." |
| Dry off hands. | "Dry hands." |
| Throw paper towel in trash can. | "Throw away paper towel. All done washing hands!" |

*Figure B.2. Washing hands*

**SKILL:**
Writing your name

**TARGETED BEHAVIORS:**
- Anchoring the paper with non-dominant hand
- Proper grasp on pencil
- Correct letter sequence

**VIDEO TYPE:**
Point-of-view Video Modeling

**LOCATION:**
Table

**MATERIALS NEEDED:**
-Table   -Paper    -Video camera
-Pencil w/ a ring of blue tape
identifying where it should be
grasped

**PEOPLE NEEDED:**
Recorder: Sarah
Actor(s): Brenna

**CAMERA LOCATION and FOCUS:**
Sarah will hold the camera next to Brenna's head and focus the camera on
Brenna's hands. Make sure to include the anchoring hand.

| Action | Scripted language |
|---|---|
| Pick up the pencil with your right hand and grasp it on the blue tape. | "Pinch blue." |
| Place your left hand on the edge of the paper to anchor it in place. | "Don't forget your helping hand." |
| Start writing the first letter and continue on with writing each following letter. | As you write each letter, say its name out loud. |
| Put the pencil down and underline the name you just wrote with your pointer finger. | Read the name out loud as you underline it. |

*Figure B.3. Skill: Writing your name*

**SKILL:**
Responding to greetings

**TARGETED BEHAVIORS:**
– Looking towards the speaker when greeted
– Saying "hi" in response to various peer or adult greetings

| VIDEO TYPE: | LOCATION: |
|---|---|
| Video Self-Modeling (VSM) | Various places throughout school (hallway, classroom, playground, and gym) |

| MATERIALS NEEDED: | PEOPLE NEEDED: |
|---|---|
| -Video camera | Recorder: Sarah<br>Actor(s): learner (Gracie), 2 familiar peers, 2 familiar adults |

**CAMERA LOCATION and FOCUS:**
Scene 1: Sarah will record the learner saying "hi" to the camera at close range.
Scenes 2-5: Sarah will separately record 2 peers and 2 adults saying "hi" to the learner. Scenes should be shot in various locations throughout the school.

| Action | Scripted language |
|---|---|
| Scene 1: Learner looks into the camera | "Hi." |
| Scene 2: (hallway) Adult 1 looks into the camera | "Hi there, Gracie!" |
| Scene 3: (classroom) Adult 2 looks into the camera | "Hello, Gracie! I'm glad you're here today." |
| Scene 4: (gym) Peer 1 looks into the camera | "Hi." |
| Scene 5: (playground) Peer 2 looks into the camera | "Hi, Gracie." |

*Figure B.4. Skill: Responding to greetings*

# SAMPLE DATA COLLECTION FORMS

Rating options:

**5**—Immediately stopped and turned toward the person calling his/her name on 1st or 2nd trial.

**4**—Stopped and turned toward the person calling his/her name within five seconds on 1st or 2nd trial.

**3**—Did not respond on 1st or 2nd trial but stopped and turned toward the person calling his/her name when it was paired with a tap on his/her shoulder on the 3rd trial.

**2**—Did not respond to the 1st, 2nd, or 3rd trial, but did stop and turn toward the person when a familiar phrase was spoken (e.g., "I'm gonna get you!" or "Where's Alery?") on the 4th trial.

**1**—Did not respond during all 4 trials.

| Date | Setting | Activity | Response | | | | Average rating |
|------|---------|----------|----------|---|---|---|----------------|
| 1/24/12 | Home | play with trains | 1 | 3 | 2 | 3 | 9/4=2.25 |
| | | | | | | | /4= |
| | | | | | | | /4= |
| | | | | | | | /4= |
| | | | | | | | /4= |
| | | | | | | | /4= |
| | | | | | | | /4= |
| | | | | | | | /4= |
| | | | | | | | /4= |
| | | | | | | | /4= |
| | | | | | | | /4= |

*Figure C.1. Data collection form. Skill: Responding to name*

Prompt options:
N Nonverbal prompt
V Verbal prompt
P Physical prompt

| Date | Setting | Play materials | Duration | Prompts given | Spontaneous play actions observed |
|------|---------|----------------|----------|---------------|-----------------------------------|
| 1/25/12 | HOME | BABY DOLL & DOCTOR TOYS | 3 MIN. | N V N V P TOTAL: 5 PROMPTS | - GAVE BABY SHOT (SEEMED REPETITIVE)<br>- PUT STETHOSCOPE ON BABY'S CHEST & MADE BEATING NOISES<br>- FED BABY W/ SPOON |
| | | | | | |
| | | | | | |
| | | | | | |
| | | | | | |
| | | | | | |

*Figure C.2. Data collection form. Skill: Independent creative play*

Student: ......................................................

Routine: ......................................................

| Date | | | | | | | | | | | | | | | | | | | |
|------|--|--|--|--|--|--|--|--|--|--|--|--|--|--|--|--|--|--|--|--|
| 1. | | | | | | | | | | | | | | | | | | | |
| 2. | | | | | | | | | | | | | | | | | | | |
| 3. | | | | | | | | | | | | | | | | | | | |
| 4. | | | | | | | | | | | | | | | | | | | |
| 5. | | | | | | | | | | | | | | | | | | | |
| 6. | | | | | | | | | | | | | | | | | | | |
| 7. | | | | | | | | | | | | | | | | | | | |
| 8. | | | | | | | | | | | | | | | | | | | |
| 9. | | | | | | | | | | | | | | | | | | | |
| 10. | | | | | | | | | | | | | | | | | | | |

Steps in the routine

P = Physicalt Prompt     V = Verbal Prompt     N = Nonverbal Prompt     I = Independent

*Figure C.3. Steps in the routine form*

Figure C.3 is a data collection tool that can be used when taking baseline and ongoing data on self-help and everyday routines at home, school, or within the community. This form can be used for routines such as brushing teeth, getting ready for bed, snack time, circle time, arriving at school, going for a walk, and many other routines.

Prior to recording data on this form, you will need to complete a task analysis to identify and sequence the steps of the routine. List the identified steps on the form. As an example, the steps of a winter routine for getting dressed to play outside in the snow are listed below:

1. Take off indoor shoes

2. Put on snow pants

3. Fasten snow pants

4. Put on snow boots

5. Put on jacket

6. Fasten jacket

7. Put on hat

8. Put on mittens

As you observe the child completing the routine, record whether the child was able to complete each step Independently (I) or with prompting. The prompts, in order from the most to least support, include Physical Prompt (P), Verbal Prompt (V), and Nonverbal Prompt (N). It is helpful to note the type of prompt the child needed in order to complete each step so you can determine if the child is making progress towards independence. Remember, it is typically easier to videotape the child doing the routine and to record data at a later time.

# REFERENCES

Bandura, A. (1977) *Social Learning Theory.* Englewood Cliffs, NJ: Prentice Hall.

Baron-Cohen, S., Leslie, A. and Frith, U. (1985) 'Does the Autistic Child Have "Theory of Mind?"' *Cognition 21,* 1, 37–46.

Bellini, S., Akullian, J. and Hopf, A. (2007) 'Increasing Social Engagement in Young Children with Autism Spectrum Disorders Using Video Self-Modeling.' *School Psychology Review 36,* 1, 80–90.

Bigelow, J., Roenblueth, A. and Wiener, N. (1943) 'Behavior, Purpose and Teleology.' *Philosophy of Science 10,* 1, 18–24.

Buggey, T. (2005) 'Applications of Video Self-Modeling with Children with Autism in a Small Private School.' *Focus on Autism and Other Developmental Disabilities 20,* 1, 180–204.

Buggey, T. (2009) *Seeing is Believing: Video Self-Modeling for People with Autism and Other Developmental Disabilities.* Bethesda, MD: Woodbine House.

Buggey, T., Hoomes, G., Sherberger, M. and Williams, S. (2011) 'Facilitating Social Initiations of Preschoolers With Autism Spectrum Disorders Using Video Self-Modeling.' *Focus on Autism and Other Developmental Disabilities 26,* 1, 25–36.

Charlop-Christy, M. and Daneshvar, S. (2003) 'Using Video Modeling to Teach Perspective Taking to Children with Autism.' *Journal of Positive Behavior Interventions 5,* 1, 12–21.

Charlop-Christy, M., Le, L. and Freeman, K. (2000) 'A Comparison of Video Modeling with In Vivo Modeling for Teaching Children with Autism.' *Journal of Autism and Developmental Disorders 30,* 6, 537–552.

Cihak, D., Smith, C., Cornett, A. and Coleman, M. (2012) 'The Use of Video Modeling With the Picture Exchange Communication System to Increase Independent Communicative Initiations in Preschoolers With Autism and Developmental Delays.' *Focus on Autism and Other Developmental Disabilities 27,* 1, 3–11.

Corbett, B. (2003) 'Video Modeling: A Window Into the World of Autism.' *The Behavior Analyst Today 4,* 3.

Corbett, B. and Abdullah, M. (2005) 'Video Modeling: Why Does It Work for Children With Autism?' *Journal of Early and Intensive Behavior Intervention 2,* 1, 2–8.

D'Ateno, P., Mangiapanello, K. and Taylor, B. (2003) 'Using Video Modeling to Teach Complex Play Sequences to a Preschooler with Autism.' *Journal of Positive Behavior Interventions 5,* 1, 5–11.

Dowrick, P. (1999) 'A Review of Self-Modeling and Related Interventions.' *Applied and Preventive Psychology 8,* 1, 23–39.

Dowrick, P. and Dove, C. (1980) 'The Use of Self-Modeling To Improve the Swimming Performance of Spina Bifida Children.' *Journal of Applied Behavior Analysis 3*, 1, 51–56.

Hepting, N. and Goldstein, H. (1996) 'Requesting by Preschoolers with Developmental Disabilities: Videotaped Self-Modeling and Learning of New Linguistic Structures.' *Topics in Early Childhood Special Education 16*, 3, 407–427.

Hine, J. and Wolery, M. (2006) 'Using Point-of-View Video Modeling to Teach Play to Preschoolers with Autism.' *Topics in Early Childhood Special Education 26*, 2, 83–93.

Jones, S. (2007) 'Imitation in Infancy: The Development of Mimicry.' *Psychological Science 18*, 7, 593–599.

Hume, K., Loftin, R. and Lantz, J. (2009) 'Increasing Independence in Autism Spectrum Disorders: A Review of Three Focused Interventions.' *Journal of Autism and Developmental Disorders 39*, 9, 1329–1338.

Lewis, M. and Brooks-Gunn, J. (1979) 'Toward a Theory of Social Cognition: The Development of Self.' *New Directions for Child and Adolescent Development 4*, 1–20.

Lord, C. and McGee, J. (eds) (2001) *Educating Children with Autism*. Washington, DC: National Academy Press.

Mahoney, G. and Perales, F. (2003) 'Using Relationship-focused Intervention to Enhance the Social-emotional Functioning of Young Children with Autism Spectrum Disorders.' *Topics in Early Childhood Special Education 23*, 2, 77–89.

Maione, L. and Mirenda, P. (2006) 'Effects of Video Modeling and Video Feedback on Peer-Directed Social Language Skills of a Child with Autism.' *Journal of Positive Behavior Interventions 8*, 2, 106–118.

Mechling, L. and Moser, S. (2010) 'Video Preference Assessment of Students with Autism for Watching Self, Adults, or Peers.' *Focus on Autism & Other Developmental Disabilities 25*, 2, 76–84.

Meltzoff, A. and Moore, M. (1977) 'Imitation of Facial and Manual Gestures by Human Neonates.' *Science: New Series 198*, 4312, 75–78.

Ozen, A., Batu, S. and Birkan, B. (2012) 'Teaching Play Skills to Children with Autism through Video Modeling: Small Group Arrangement and Observational Learning.' *Education and Training in Autism and Developmental Disabilities 47*, 1, 84–96.

Schertz, H. and Odom, S. (2007) 'Promoting Joint Attention in Toddlers with Autism: A Parent-Mediated Developmental Model.' *Journal of Autism and Developmental Disorders 37*, 8, 1562–1575.

Schön, D. (1983) *The Reflective Practitioner: How Professionals Think in Action*. London: Temple Smith.

Shattuck, P., Durkin, M., Maennar, M., Newschaffer, C. *et al.* (2009) 'Timing of Identification Among Children With an Autism Spectrum Disorder: Findings From a Population-based Surveillance Study.' *Journal of the American Academy of Child and Adolescent Psychiatry 48*, 5, 474–483.

Tretreault, A. and Lerman, D. (2010) 'Teaching Social Skills to Children With Autism using Point-of-view Video Modeling.' *Education and Treatment of Children 33*, 3, 395–419.

United States Copyright Office (2004) *Individuals With Disabilities Improvement Act of 2004*. Washington, DC: United States Copyright Office. Available at www.copyright.gov/legislation/pl108-446.pdf, accessed on 23 March 2012.

Video Modeling: Overview (2010) *The National Professional Development Center on Autism Spectrum Disorders*. Madison, WI: Video Modeling: Overview. Available at http://autismpdc.fpg.unc.edu/content/video-modeling, accessed on 8 March 2012.

Wetherby, A. and Woods, J. (2006) 'Early Social Interaction Project for Children with Autism Spectrum Disorders Beginning in the Second Year of Life: A Preliminary Study.' *Topics in Early Childhood Special Education 26*, 2, 67–82.

Winner, M. (2007) *Thinking About You, Thinking About Me*. 2nd Edition. San Jose, CA: Think Social Publishing, Inc.

# INDEX

CPI Antony Rowe
Eastbourne, UK
October 23, 2019